idney Earle Smith

The career of Sidney Earle Smith, Dean of Law, Dalhousie University (1929–34), President of the University of Manitoba (1934–44), President of the University of Toronto (1945–59), had a variety of backgrounds which were significant in determining his impressive achievement in Canada's humanistic tradition. He was reared in the vigorous landscape and living of the Maritimes, rigorously trained in the discipline of the law whose traditions he always enjoyed and respected, challenged and stimulated by very different but equally significant administrative problems as president first of a struggling Western university (Manitoba), and then of the largest and most complex in Canada (Toronto), and finally was caught up in the compelling swirl of international politics from the office of Secretary of State for External Affairs. At every stage of these activities Sidney Smith made an indelible impression on his associates. One of these, who knew him intimately in the work of the Canadian Association for Adult Education, is the author of this short but revealing biography.

Mr. Corbett has carefully and vividly sketched in the backgrounds of his subject's story, has woven into the account with ingenious informality reminiscences of the man and his work by a goodly company of his colleagues, and has brought out personality, style, methods, beliefs in a persuasive atmosphere of personal warmth and strong academic conviction. This is a book of lively charm to read, and also a valuable recording of a public servant who "left a mark upon his time and his country that the passage of the years will further illuminate." Its initial appearance in the year of the opening of Sidney Smith Hall, built to house the Faculty of Arts whose interests he had always served with sturdy devotion, is a happy association.

E. A. CORBETT is himself a Maritimer, born in Truro, N.S. He graduated from McGill University, served overseas in World War I, and then joined the star For the University of Alberta. He became the Director of its Department of Extension (1928–1936) and then served as Director of the Canadian Association for Adult Education (1936–1951). He is the author, among other books, of a biography of another leading figure in Canadian education, Henry Marshall Tory.

SIDNEY
EARLE
SMITH

E. A. Corbett

UNIVERSITY OF TORONTO PRESS

University of Toronto Press

Diamond Anniversary 1961

Contents

Sidney Earle Smith

CHAPTER ONE *Beginnings*

ONE RAINY SUNDAY IN JUNE 1960 I SAT WITH MR. P. W. SMITH
in the living-room of his trim white house on upper Main
Street of the village of Port Hood, Cape Breton, while he told
me about the ancestors and the boyhood of the late Hon.
Sidney Earle Smith, Secretary of State for External Affairs for
Canada. P. W. Smith, a second cousin of Sidney's, is a retired
Supervisor of Fisheries and has spent a great deal of his spare
time during the past twenty years compiling an exhaustive
record of the families that came into Cape Breton on the first
wave of the United Empire Loyalist migration. His record
makes special reference of the Smith family who came to Cape
Breton from Cape Cod, Massachusetts, in 1786.

Mr. Smith's house looks out over the narrow strait that
separates the island of Port Hood from the mainland on which
the village stands. Through the fog and the rain we could just
see the whale-shaped hump of land which had been the home
of Sidney Smith's ancestors for more than one hundred years.
In the days of the French régime that little island had been an
important shipping and boat-building centre and at its southern
end were the immense stone quarries which provided most, if
not all, of the stone for the building of the great fort at Louisburg. The stone was cut and shaped according to specification
on the island and then transported by boat through the Strait

of Canso and up the eastern shore of Cape Breton to Louisburg. Today the island is the home of some fifteen or twenty families of fishermen, just as it was when Sidney Smith was a small boy. Most of the old homes are there. But most of the Smiths have gone, their places taken by prosperous young commercial fishermen whose family cars are parked at the village waterfront, while traffic across the strait is now by fast sea-going motor-boat. The beauty of the island remains.

When Captain David Smith moved from Cape Cod, Massachusetts, to Port Hood in the year 1786 he brought with him his wife and five sons, Lewis, David, Isaac, Parker, and Harding. At that time Port Hood Island was referred to in original surveys as "Juste au Corps"—up to the waist—which would seem to indicate that the island at one time during the French occupation was joined to the mainland by a sand-bar. The Scottish settlers later called it Chestico—obviously a corruption of Juste au Corps. Captain Smith settled on land at the south end of the island, where two more children, Rebecca and John, were born within the next three years. But Captain Smith was not to enjoy his new-found freedom for very long. Three years after his arrival at Port Hood he was out one day with two of his sons seal-hunting on the ice when the field broke up and they were marooned on an ice-floe about two hundred yards from shore and drifting slowly towards the open sea. The father told his sons to stay on the ice while he swam ashore to get a boat. The sons watched their father, swimming strongly, make his way through the broken ice-field until he reached the shore, but as he tried to pull himself out of the water his strength failed and he sank beneath the surface never to reappear. The sons remained on the ice-floe and were picked up next day several miles northward near Cape Mabou. Shortly after her husband's death, Captain Smith's widow, Rebecca, obtained from the Crown a grant of five hundred acres of land on Port Hood Island, and the ancestors of Sidney Smith occupied this property from 1792 to 1911.

Three of the sons of Captain David Smith—Lewis, David, and Isaac—took up grants of land on the mainland, while Parker and John settled on Port Hood Island on land granted to them by their mother. Here the Smiths' daughter Rebecca married Miles McDaniel; they settled at Margaree, and their descendants have been among the most distinguished people of Nova Scotia: judges, priests, and bishops, many of whom graduated from St. Francis Xavier University. The Port Hood Island families grouped their houses in a small settlement on its northern end on a knoll surrounded by trees, overlooking Port Hood harbour. The house in which Sidney was later to be born and spend his youth was a two-storey frame house with shingled roof and walls, two brick flues, four bedrooms, a large kitchen, a dining room, parlour and other rooms. The farm consisted of approximately twenty acres with ten acres under cultivation. The livestock usually consisted of four or five cows, one horse, fifteen head of sheep, and about twenty hens. Belonging to the farm were a barn and other buildings big enough to house the stock and to provide storage for hay, oats, and other feed for the animals.

Sidney's father, John P. Smith, who was a grandson of Captain David Smith, carried on commercial fishing for lobsters, cod, haddock, herring, and mackerel from May through to December at which time the harbour and the strait between the island and the mainland were frozen over. His earnings from this operation would usually be between five and seven hundred dollars a year. The farm was cultivated not so much for income as to yield food—milk and butter, poultry and eggs—for the family. There was always a young heifer or steer and a pig or two for butchering in the fall, and a winter's supply of potatoes, turnips, cabbage, beets, and parsnips was stored away with barrels of salted cod, haddock, and herring. Even the forests and the pasture-land contributed to the family food supply with beech and hazel nuts, partridge and rabbits from the bush, and wild ducks from the marshes.

Strawberries, raspberries, blueberries, and blackberries were available for preserving. Food was never a problem in any Cape Breton home where the people were willing to work. In many homes in the Maritime provinces as late as the early years of this century, wool from the sheep was carded, spun, and woven into cloth on the farm. A cobbler came around once a year to fit the family for shoes. My own father, who was a Presbyterian minister with eight children and a salary of 750 dollars a year, had a complete cobbling outfit and our winter moccasins were made in his workshop, as were all repairs to our "boughten" shoes.

In 1884 John Parker Smith married Margaret Jane Etheridge, a school-teacher from the Margaree Valley. Her ancestors, both English and Scotch, experienced great hardship on their Atlantic crossing and, after landing on Cape Breton, settled inland from the sea in that quiet valley. The bride was a remarkable woman who, to the day of her death in 1945 at the age of eighty-eight, retained all her faculties. She had outlived her husband by more than twenty years. "Vitality and humour and shrewdness were combined in her with an uncanny ability to see through people. Nothing amused her more than to detect sham and humbug, but instead of bemoaning the wickedness and folly of the world, she treated it as a source of wit and laughter. She was apparently a woman with a genius for management. Improvement and change intrigued her, and she was convinced that the next generation must be an advance on the old. It was obvious to everyone around Port Hood that John Smith had gotten himself a wife who was full of the joy of living."[1] They made a handsome couple as photographs taken at the close of the last century clearly show: the mother's face full of character and imagination; the father's just and kind as his children now chiefly remember him, a man of medium height with clear-cut features, a bold

[1]Professor George Wilson of Dalhousie.

moustache, and a finely shaped head with an abundance of brown hair that he kept throughout his life.

Both parents had a profound effect on the thinking and the aspirations of their children. The mother probably had a greater influence upon Sidney's career than any other person. She had set her heart on his training for the Methodist ministry, but when it became apparent that her son's interests lay elsewhere, she made no complaint. The parents had grown up schooled in the Cape Breton way of life and were self-reliant, fiercely independent, deeply religious, and profound believers in the virtues of hard work. Like most Cape Breton people, they had always lived close to nature. As Neil MacNeil puts it in *The Highland Heart in Nova Scotia*:

The Cape Breton people could fend for themselves as could the flowers in the meadow, the fox in the brakes and the trout in the deep pools. Such people seem to have a special endowment from the God of Creation who cares for his own. They have a calm that the people of the city can seldom acquire, a simplicity that is close to the sublime and a fortitude that belittles the adversities of this life. Men and women went on living from youth to venerable old age, never wealthy and never really poor, seldom troubled, and never released from work.[2]

In John Parker Smith's home the everyday work of the house and the farm, the catching and processing of fish had changed little in a hundred years of practice. The young people grew up with the skills, the craftsmanship, and the inherited instincts which made them sure of hand and foot on the land or in a fishing dory on the open sea. The sons learned farming, fishing, hunting, carpentry, and blacksmithing from their fathers and the daughters learned cooking, sewing, and in some instances weaving, canning, and preserving, and the care of children from their mothers.

Thus John Smith's family of four—Frank, Myrtle, Maude, and young Sidney—grew up and got the kind of practical

[2]Neil MacNeil, *The Highland Heart in Nova Scotia* (Toronto and New York, 1958), p. 34.

training that readied them for life and whatever vicissitudes it might bring. Years later I heard Sidney Smith, then President of the University of Toronto, speaking at a meeting of labour leaders, say, "I knew the smell of the bilge in a fishing boat before I could read."

In addition to the formal teaching of the small one-room school nearby, the Smith children were guided in their reading and their thinking by both parents. Their father had his skills as a fisherman-farmer, as carpenter and boat-builder, but he was also a diligent reader and a life-long student of astronomy. Their mother continued to use her training as a school-teacher to good avail. Both parents had a firm belief in education and much study of the King James Version of the Bible had given them an instinctive taste for good literature and whatsoever things are true and of good report. The older people to whom the children listened in their homes or along the wharves and in the fields had "a wisdom and a philosophy of their own. For the most part they knew little about the history, the sciences or the ways of thinking of the modern world but in their own way they knew more than most scholars for they understood nature in all its moods."[3] And, in all Cape Breton-ers, often hidden under a grim and forbidding exterior, is a sense of humour that has given that lovely country a body of folk tales unequalled anywhere in Canada.

The Smith children all took their share of the work in the house and on the farm, but their schooling came first. This was the decision of both parents and as soon as they were through with the one-room school on the island, they crossed the strait to Port Hood every morning in the summer to attend Port Hood Academy. In the winter when the harbour was frozen over they boarded in the village. Ever since I had first met Sidney Smith I had heard—not from him, but from newspaper articles—about his crossing the open sea in a row-

[3]*Ibid.*, p. 34.

boat to attend the school, and I used to think of a small ten-year-old struggling with a fishing dory across a mile of choppy water. Actually there were always other youngsters attending the Academy and there were usually three or four of them in the boat. But they were skilled in handling any kind of sea-going craft and would think little of crossing the strait alone if it were necessary to do so.

"We weren't bad students," said P. W. Smith, "but Sid was miles ahead of the rest of us. He had a queer curiosity about everything and he would never be satisfied to just sit and listen to the teachers. He was always asking questions. He wanted to know the why and the wherefore of everything and, mind you, we had some of the finest teachers in Nova Scotia at Port Hood Academy. When Sid was down here not long before his death, he came up here and made a speech and he sat in that chair there till three o'clock in the morning talking over the old days and he said that Miss Ida Tompkins was one of the best teachers he ever had, anywhere. But don't get the idea that young Sid Smith was a saint by any means. He was as full of fun and mischief as any of us, and like most of us he would sometimes skimp on his homework. I remember one time when we were both quite small calling for Sid to go fishing, but he was up on the roof of the back verandah. His mother had put him up there and taken the ladder away so he couldn't get down till he'd finished his sums and his spelling; but at school he mastered in two or three gulps what it took the rest of us days to understand."

In 1911 John Smith made what must have been a painful decision. Frank, the eldest of the family, had completed his high school education and was in training as an accountant; of the two girls, Myrtle was at business college in Halifax and Maude was in the upper grade, but Sidney at fourteen years of age was ready for the university. After much thought and probably long discussion it was decided to sell the old home with all its history and family memories to settle in Windsor where the youngest member of the family could attend King's College.

In May 1911 John Smith bought a house and six acres of land just outside the town of Windsor on the highway to Halifax. The house is a two-storey white clapboard building with ample room for a family of six, and the six acres, mostly orchard, stretch along the base of a hill parallel to the highway. Here John Smith farmed his small holding to provide food and earned his living as a carpenter. I called at the house last summer and talked with a neighbour, a retired carpenter who worked with Smith on many buildings. "He was a fine man," he said, "and a first-rate carpenter. One day we were working on a roof in the town there. It was a terrible hot day and Mr. Smith turned to me and said, 'Would you work in this heat for yourself?' And I said 'No, I wouldn't.' 'Well then,' he said, 'let's go home.' Young Sid walked to King's College from here summer and winter—it's only about a mile and a half. He was a bright and jolly kid with a smile and a wave of the hand for all of us. He used to work in a store in town there every time he had time off from school. I think he went on surveys too. I guess he pretty well paid his way as he went along."

Sidney Earle Smith was a young man in a hurry. He finished his Arts course and had taken his B.A. by the spring of 1915 and was ready for his first year in Law at Dalhousie. Meanwhile he had articled with Judge Sangster of Windsor. F. W. Walsh, Deputy Minister of Agriculture for Nova Scotia, took me to call on the Judge who not long before our visit had celebrated his ninetieth birthday. He welcomed us into the study in his fine old house high on a hill overlooking the town and with the Bay of Fundy plainly visible in the distance.

"Sidney Smith," he said. "Yes, he articled with me when he was about eighteen, I think, and a fine young fellow he was.

Wait, I've got a picture of him here standing outside my office; fine looking, very happy and good-natured young man. I had six clerks most of the time. He was one of the best I ever had— quick to learn, always agreeable, earnest, reliable, honourable and efficient. Well, I was on the bench for 60 years and I used to think I had reached the point where I could tell by the way a man walked what kind of a character he was. Sidney Smith as I knew him was a happy youth and inherently kind. If he had to be tough sometimes, and who doesn't, especially a man in a position of great responsibility—if he had to be tough it was because the occasion called for firmness and even then he wouldn't like it."

By the time Sidney was ready for the Dalhousie Law School in August 1915 war had broken out and first-year men watched their seniors prepare for enlistment in the Canadian forces. His great friend at that time was a fellow student, R. E. Inglis, now a Halifax magistrate. I had no knowledge of Sidney's war record; in many evenings spent with him in hotel rooms during his two-year presidency of the Canadian Association for Adult Education, I never heard him refer to his part in World War I. But a letter from Mr. Inglis indicates that early in 1916 he and Sid began to think about enlisting. Sidney's brother, Frank, had already been in France on active service for two years and many of their student friends were joining up. Early in May the two young men joined the Royal Canadian Garrison Artillery for a course in siege artillery work and became inmates of the ancient stone barracks within the walls of Citadel Hill. During the next two months they trained in signalling and the duties of a Battery Commander's Assistant, generally referred to as a B.C.A. On September 26, No. 8 Canadian Siege Battery sailed for England; there it was stationed at Witley Camp and the Battery's number was subsequently changed to No. 9. After training at various camps in England the unit arrived in France and went into action a few days later, previous to and during the battle of Vimy Ridge which began on April 9. From then on, up to and including Passchendaele, the No. 9 Siege Battery was in almost constant action. During the years 1916–18 Bob Inglis and Sidney Smith were inseparable. In France and Belgium they shared the same billets and often the same blankets. The morning Smith left the battery to take his training in the R.A.F. it was Inglis who woke him at daylight and stayed with him until he moved off in an army lorry on his way to England and the life of a flyer. There are no friendships more deep and lasting than those forged in the heat of battle, but it was typical of both these young Nova Scotians that the story of their war experiences is told without drum-beating and their parting on that summer morning in 1918 after two years of close comradeship was as casual as a work-day greeting.

The Armistice was made before Sidney Smith's training in the R.A.F. was completed. A photograph taken of him in France shows him in the tight-fitting, neat uniform of a gunner, tall (5 ft. 11½ in.), slim, and with the tough wiry body of a soldier who has seen hard service. He was an unusually handsome young man with fine even features, a heavy head of light brown hair, a countenance glowing with health and goodwill and the warm friendly smile for which he was famous all his life. One can almost hear his familiar greeting, "Well, bless your heart; how are you!"

Early in 1919 Smith returned to Canada, went immediately to his home in Windsor, and while working in Judge Sangster's office as a clerk finished his work for the M.A. degree at King's College. During his B.A. course at King's he had taken classes in Crimes, Contracts, and Torts and when he entered the Dalhousie Law School he was given credit for these subjects. In the fall of 1919 he again entered Dalhousie Law School. During the two terms he spent at Dalhousie, 1915–16 and 1919–20, he wrote examinations in twenty-one subjects and was awarded a First in each.

After graduation, at the suggestion of Dean MacRae of the Dalhousie Law School, whose influence and inspiration were always carefully considered, Smith did a year's postgraduate work at Harvard, with the assurance from Dean MacRae that when he returned he would have a teaching post in the Dalhousie Law School. How he financed this undertaking is not clear, but undoubtedly the family helped and his well-known habit of always paying his debts promptly and meticulously is guarantee enough that every cent of a loan from whatever source would be paid back. The family was close-knit, undemonstrative, but more than ordinarily devoted to each other, and it is certain that a way would be found to achieve anything on which the younger brother set his heart.

On his return from Harvard, Smith was appointed Lecturer and later Assistant Professor in the Dalhousie Law School where he was soon recognized as a sound teacher with a first-class mind. "One thing you can never stress too much about Sidney Smith," says his friend Professor George Wilson of Dalhousie, "was his capacity for work. To that there was apparently no limit. His health was excellent and he never seemed to tire. His geniality and natural kindness drew students and professors alike to his door." From 1925 to 1929 he was Lecturer at Osgoode Hall, Toronto. Then, in 1929, at thirty-two years of age, he was appointed Dean of the Dalhousie Law School, one of the most distinguished law schools in North America. It had been founded in 1883. Its first Dean, Professor R. C. Weldon, had continued as head of the faculty for thirty-one years and in those years, to quote Angus L. MacDonald, Premier of Nova Scotia, "He gave it personality, and he gave it distinction. He made it not merely a Law School but a breeding ground for public service and public men."[4] In its fifty years of history the school had turned out over 700 graduates among whom were many who filled the highest

[4]From an address given at the Fiftieth Anniversary celebrations of the founding of the Dalhousie Law School in 1934.

offices of the Judiciary and the State. Two Prime Ministers of Canada (Sir John Thompson and R. B. Bennett), Judges of the Supreme Court of Canada, and Judges and Chief Justices in the provinces have passed through its halls.

In his five years as Dean, Smith renewed all his old friendships and, as the school stories indicate, not only added greatly to the fine traditions of Dalhousie's Law Faculty but added liveliness and excitement as well. Even when he was Dean his sense of fun often overcame his official bearing and at Dalhousie his friends still tell of his riding a bicycle through the corridor of the Law building in full academic regalia. Except on special occasions, he cared nothing for dignity, says Professor Wilson. "What he loved when off duty was noise and movement and fun.

"One of his favourite sports was playing volleyball at the Y.M.C.A. gymnasium. There he was always the noisiest man on the floor. As soon as he arrived in the gym everybody knew it. Sid Smith had arrived, now something would happen.

"One of the leading lawyers in Newfoundland at the present time is a man by the name of McIvoy. Before he entered the Dalhousie Law School he had to complete a year in Arts. He came around to see me one night about it. I received him at the door and took him into our living-room where a fight (or apparent fight) was in progress. Two men were rolling around on the floor. I said, 'The man on the bottom is a professor in the Law School. The man on top is the Dean of the Law School.' There was always a great big romping boy inside him. He liked practical jokes, fun, noise, movement. Yet even when he acted most outrageously, when you thought that he had turned into a wild Indian, he could sober up instantly if the occasion demanded it. He was always master of himself."

In 1926 came what Sidney always referred to as the luckiest day in his life. In that year he met Harriet Rand. She came from Canning, Nova Scotia, was a niece of Sir Robert Borden, and was working in a bank in Halifax when they met. She was tall, slender, with fair hair, blue eyes, classic features, and an expression of quiet dignity and charm which was to distinguish her throughout life. They were married the same year and went to Paris for their honeymoon. Their married life was idyllic throughout and Harriet Smith's loyalty, charm, and good judgment were a constant strength and inspiration to her husband.

Meanwhile Dean Smith had become a part of the life of Halifax and of the province. As the twenty-second President of the Y.M.C.A., he worked night and day to organize large numbers of civic committees to deal with the enormous task of caring for the hundreds of unemployed who were flocking to the city. From 1931 to 1933 he met regularly with the executive officers, club leaders, programme organizers, and staff to co-ordinate a vigorous and wholesome plan of Association services. He was for five years a member of the Commission on Uniformity of Legislation in Canada, assistant editor of the *Canadian Bar Review*, Chairman of the Faculty of the Conservatory of Music, Governor of the Halifax Ladies' College, and had somewhere found time to publish three books: *Cases on Trusts, Cases on Equity* with Professor H. E. Read, and *Manual of Canadian Business Law* with Dean J. D. Falconbridge.

To an unusual degree he had won the attachment of the students. So much so that amid the flood of newspaper comment and regret that followed the announcement of his appointment as President of the University of Manitoba, the undergraduate paper headlined its tribute "Smitty Leaving Dalhousie—What Do We Do Now?"

Early in the summer of 1934, Dean Smith received a letter from Mr. D. C. Coleman, then Vice-President of the Canadian Pacific Railway Company at Winnipeg, and Chairman of the Board of Governors of the University of Manitoba. The letter contained transportation to Vancouver and return and an invitation to meet him in Vancouver, at a time agreed upon, where Mr. Coleman would be on his annual inspection tour. Dean Smith's reaction to the interview is best told by Mr. F. W. Crawford who was Comptroller of the University of Manitoba and Sidney Smith's intimate friend during his Presidency of that institution.

"Coleman was a small man physically, and he was very formal. He used words more sparingly than any man of high position whom I have met during my lifetime. He appeared to be so careful of the number of words used that, if he used ten you would almost think that he was saying to himself, 'I used two words more than I should have done.' However, each word counted, and the meaning of what he had to say was rarely, if ever, in doubt.

"On arrival in Vancouver, Sidney arranged to meet the high railway executive who was also Chairman of the Board of Governors of the University of Manitoba. When they met, Coleman was very courteous, but he was not very communicative. He gave Sidney about twenty minutes of his time and dismissed him politely, but firmly, with the matter of the Presidency still uncertain in Sidney's mind. Was Coleman impressed with the candidate? Sidney did not know, and he was, to say the least, slightly upset. During the interview, Coleman said little about the position, but he did discuss salary to some extent, and a few of the more pressing problems. Sidney said, 'Imagine if you can, travelling 4,000 miles to meet the man who was looking for a new President of the University of Manitoba, and being granted a twenty-minute interview.'

"I first met Sidney when he was on his way back from Vancouver, after he met Mr. Coleman. He stopped at Winnipeg to meet the other members of the Board, and he spent considerable time with me. I took him through the University buildings and I showed him the house in which he would live.

He was not unimpressed with the buildings and equipment, and he liked the house. It was a very good house, but it was dirty and needed decorating badly. I quickly made a deal with him about decorating the house. Sidney said, 'We will leave it to you, Walter; we will be quite satisfied if you choose neutral colours; get your wife to help you out and everything will be fine.' He was not an exacting man or a demanding man where his own interests were concerned. The University was in financial trouble, and this attitude made a great hit with me. I remember him as a very attractive young man, whose enthusiasm continually bubbled over. That enthusiasm, and his bright and cheerful smile, were also apparent throughout the ten years that I worked with him, despite many difficulties and frustrations for one who was anxious to expand and develop the University."

If Sidney Smith was disturbed by what he saw of a once great University he gave no evidence of it. He seemed to delight in the challenge the situation presented. He was the kind of man who was always interested in what comes next. It would demand all his talents—his enormous energy, tact, and good judgment—to restore confidence in an organization whose staff was disheartened and disorganized and in which the people of the province had lost faith. He returned to Halifax and resigned his position as Dean of the Law Faculty.

There followed a round of official and informal banquets and farewell parties for Dean Smith and his wife, both of whom had won the admiration and affection of the University staff and students and of the community. On one of these occasions the Dean made a statement which was characteristic of the man and his working philosophy:

I am not taking with me any educational policy designed in Halifax for Manitoba. Any successful university policy must be related to the time and place of the particular institution. I will endeavour to take with me, as other sons of Dalhousie have done, a resolution to give of my best in fair thinking, square dealing, hard work, common sense and devotion to the institution and the community which she serves.

He was leaving behind him all the friends of his youth and of his undergraduate days and his fellow academicians, to undertake at thirty-seven years of age the most difficult task he had ever faced. But he had the satisfaction of knowing that his work at Dalhousie had been well done. In the Dalhousie Law School with its proud traditions Sidney Earle Smith had proved himself as a teacher and a scholar. Now he must turn his talents to the re-establishment and administration of a great university. He was confident he could do it.

CHAPTER TWO   *Western Record*

IN JULY 1934 DEAN SMITH LEFT HALIFAX WITH HIS WIFE AND TWO small daughters to take up his new duties as President of the University of Manitoba. In order to understand something of the nature of the job he had undertaken, one must keep in mind the extraordinary difficulties into which the University had fallen. In 1932 it was discovered that the Bursar of the University, who was also Chairman of the Board of Governors, had been guilty of misusing funds and the loss to the University was close to one million dollars. The following year the Provincial Grant had been cut from $500,000 to $250,000. Teachers' salaries were reduced by about 25 per cent in most cases and all members of staff were placed on a tenure of one year. Fees payable by students were raised at a time when parents were least able to pay them. Enrolment had fallen off badly through lack of employment during summer months and because of advanced fees. In a letter Robert England, then Western Manager of the Department of Colonization and Agriculture for the Canadian National Railways and President of the Winnipeg Canadian Club, says: "The bleak, dismal, temporary huts on Broadway, the difficulties of transportation in below zero temperature between the St. Vital site and Broadway; dispersion of library facilities; the lack of cohesion; the latent dispute as to aims, secular or religious, and the inability of the Province to give financial support in the depression, the lack of endowment—all these were handicaps enough, but the loss of such funds as existed plunged the institution into a slough of despond in which confidence in the administration had disappeared."

In 1933 a new Board of Governors had been appointed with Mr. D. C. Coleman, a Vice-President of the Canadian Pacific Railway Company, as Chairman and Mr. Justice A. K. Dysart of the Manitoba Court of King's Bench, Vice-Chairman. The first step in the reorganization was to appoint F. W. Crawford, a member of the Board of Governors, as full-time Comptroller and Secretary of the Board. Mr. Crawford was a graduate of the institution and, to quote Professor W. L. Morton, "He brought to his duties a rough vigour, a fine administrative gift, an unusual sense of the unity of the University and a rare devotion to its interests. . . . The new organization of the financial administration was to give the board assurance of sound management of university funds and to free the president from responsibility for the same."[1] Fortunately for all concerned the Comptroller and the new President soon became fast friends and, although both could be stubborn and differences were bound to occur between two strong-minded men, in a letter to the writer, Walter Crawford states quite simply, "I loved the man."

The new President was received with great enthusiasm by the press, the public, and his university colleagues. Maritimers had a good reputation as presidents of Canadian universities. There had been Dawson at McGill, Grant and Gordon at Queen's, Falconer at Toronto, Murray at Saskatchewan, and Tory at Alberta. Here by the grace of God was another one— young, jovial, good to look at, with something of the West in his smile and his hearty greeting, even in the way he wore

[1]W. L. Morton, *One University: A History of the University of Manitoba 1877–1952* (Toronto: McClelland and Stewart Limited, 1957), pp. 154–5.

his hat. It might be, they said, it just might be that with his kind of academic background, he has "come to his kingdom for such a time as this."

To a *Winnipeg Free Press* reporter who interviewed the new President shortly after his arrival, he explained that since he had never been a university president before and since his name was Smith, spelled with an "i," he should not be expected to take himself too seriously. He spoke of his lovely Cape Breton homeland and the new kind of beauty he had already found in the Western landscape, of the divided devotion already claiming him, and quoted to emphasize his point from James Gillis, the Cape Breton poet:

> Here's to thee, Queen Victoria
> In all your bright regalia,
> With one foot in Canada
> And the other in Australia.[2]

He went on to say that top students in universities are not always the ones who make the grade in business or public affairs. In fact, he said, there is a saying at Harvard Law School that the Grade A students make the laws, the Grade B students make the judges, and the Grade C students make the money.

The big house on the Fort Garry campus, which was the home of the President, with its charming hostess, Harriet Smith, became the centre of social life on the campus. He was surrounded by goodwill in the University and in the city, and the affectionate regard of the Chancellor, J. W. Dafoe, of Mr. Justice Dysart, Chairman of the Board of Governors, and of his working colleagues was a source of strength to him.

Within a few months of his arrival in Winnipeg, indeed, he had so impressed the Chancellor that from that time on, in spite of their political differences of opinion, they had such a genuine affection for each other that "they shared just about

[2]There is some doubt whether James Gillis is the author of these lines or not. They have been attributed to James Gay also.

everything, the University, politics, and all."[3] It soon became apparent to others too that this jovial man with the disarming smile was a first-class administrator. Watson Thomson, Director of Extension at the University from 1940 to 1944 points out that Smith had an extraordinary capacity to "sense the nub of a problem and to quickly map out the most effective line of attack on it. . . . His performance as a committee chairman was a sheer joy to watch. Call it skill in manipulation if you like, but it's a mighty useful skill in the kind of world we live in. He had a combination of speed and artistry in it which one watched with the same kind of delight evoked by an expert potter at work. I think of his extraordinary warmth, thoughtfulness and general likability. The ideological gulf between Sid and myself was wide enough in all conscience, yet, not only did he never inhibit me in doing my job as I thought it ought to be done, but he was unfailingly supportive to the point of genuine friendship. He had real magnanimity."[4] It is worth noting at this point that at the Conservative convention in Winnipeg in the fall of 1942, the Hon. Mr. Meighen in his address to the delegates made a bitter attack on the Canadian Broadcasting Corporation with particular reference to the regular weekly broadcasts of Watson Thomson. I asked Mr. Walter Crawford about this and he replied, "Neither the President nor anyone else in the University paid any attention to the attack."

Professor Morton sums it up:

Dr. Smith possessed all the qualities of the new type of president which was emerging in Canadian universities, the administrator president, flexible to the ways of the world, yet still academically acceptable—"a reconciler of irreconcilables," as President Klinck of the University of British Columbia was to say in welcome to the new president. President Smith brought the University of Manitoba the very things it needed: confidence, leadership and presence. His coming raised hopes his term of office was to

[3]G. V. Ferguson, personal communication.
[4]Watson Thomson, personal communication.

realize. . . . When he was inaugurated in October, 1934, he made a declaration of faith which did much to bring the thoughts of the members and friends of the university back from their preoccupation with mere survival to those things which alone made survival meaningful. He began by stressing the need to preserve the primacy of the liberal spirit in education, in all branches of study and especially in the liberal arts, its native home. Without the preservation and encouragement of an able and devoted faculty, he declared, no university could flourish. But, its inner life secured, the university must recognize and fulfil its many responsibilities to the society it served and which maintained it.[5]

There is no space here to set down the complete text of this first major address as President of the University of Manitoba. In the opinion of the writer it is certainly one of the best of Sidney Smith's career and one of the best statements regarding the function of a university I have seen anywhere. His answer to the question, "What is the function of a University?" was:

The obvious answer is that its function is to teach. This is good enough as far as it goes, but it does not go far enough. A university is a mechanism for the diffusion of knowledge and also a centre where the fields of knowledge are being explored. The imparting of information is an important objective but it is the minor part of the university's obligation to the student. An Oxford teacher has said that education is what remains after you have forgotten all you have learned—the real residuum is the mental discipline, the keen understanding, the power to discriminate and judge and the capacity to proceed directly from a fixed point to valid conclusions, and perhaps above all, the appreciation of the fact that one knows very little. One may obtain information from a good encyclopaedia but the toughness of mind which enables a person to sift out random theories, empty shibboleths, lasting paradoxes, and imposing sophistries may only be gained from hard schooling.

As Professor Morton has pointed out, this was the sort of thing the Manitoba people wanted to hear and it had the effect of restoring confidence and rallying the friends of the University to its support.

[5]W. L. Morton, *One University: A History of the University of Manitoba 1877–1952*, pp. 159–60.

For the Alumni the new President had a special message:

Experiences of several western states' universities has shown that the Alumni are great workers when it comes to promoting football stadiums, building bell-towers and erecting ornamental gates, but when it comes to maintaining bursaries for investigating the eating habits of Myoxococus Digilatus [sic] they simply do not respond. . . . They take it for granted that the state, which means the taxpayers, will pay for all the vital activities of the university, while they decorate dear old Alma Mater with ornaments and try to make sure that athletic prowess is up to snuff. The system is not likely to work well in Manitoba. The Province staggering under a heavy funded debt will not for some time to come be able to make large contributions to the University. The institution must continue to be to a large extent self-supporting and at the same time must enlarge the opportunities for effective work by gifted students. There is only one way in which this can be done, and that is by increasing the number of scholarships. The Alumni are in the logical position to take the lead in this phase of the University's development.

During his first year the President laboured to get to know the people of the province and spent many week-ends in small towns and rural communities exchanging ideas with farmers and business men. Soon after his appointment as President, he had realized, as did all of his colleagues, that perhaps the greatest weakness in the institution was its lack of a widely based public support. From the beginning of their histories the universities of Saskatchewan and Alberta had recognized the necessity of relating the thinking and the research going on within the university to the economic and social needs of the taxpayers. But they were from the beginning state-supported institutions with centralized authority, whereas the University of Manitoba was formed in 1877 by the federation of three existing colleges, St. Boniface (Roman Catholic), St. John's (Anglican), and Manitoba (Presbyterian). The succession of constitutional changes which eventually led to a more centralized university administration is too involved to include in a brief sketch of this kind. The fact is that there had always been a wide gap between the mass of the people of the province and the University itself. This was a situation that the new administration determined to correct. All were agreed that a university supported by a provincial government can only be secure if the people who pay the taxes are convinced that the institution has value to the community and to individuals. The new President set himself the task of regaining for the University the confidence and the loyalty of the people of the province. He undertook to address public meetings at farmers' conventions, country fairs, in community halls, church basements, country school-houses, wherever and whenever he was invited to do so. No request was beneath his notice. Summer and winter he made himself available.

It was deadly work, as any extension worker can testify, but Smith loved every minute of it. He had always enjoyed meeting people, particularly people of the soil and the sea. Here he was at his best. On occasions such as these his speech was simple, unpretentious, and direct. Very often his best work was done after the lecture was over as he swapped yarns in the hotel late at night or mingled with his audience over a cup of tea following the meeting. Gradually he built back into the civic consciousness the feeling that "this chap is one of us and the University is a going concern after all, and of vital concern to all of us."

Stories began to circulate about his free and easy manner and his love of a joke. When such stories begin about a university president in Western Canada, particularly if they are folksy and amusing, the president is on his way to a solid position with the public. There were good-natured yarns about his amused reaction to the informality of the Comptroller, Walter Crawford, whose habit it was to bring in the University's Annual Report, throw it on the President's desk and say, "There are all the facts and figures. Now you shovel in the slush." To which the President replied, "Salt on the mackerel we call it in Cape Breton—makes it more palatable." His easy manner prompted his audiences to similar spontaneity. Once when addressing a meeting of farmers in a small town community hall, he told of the economist who said, "There is nothing wrong with Manitoba except too much heat and too little water." Whereupon someone in Smith's audience shouted, "That's all that's wrong with Hell."

In the city, he took an interest in the arts. He backed the Department of Architecture and Fine Art and the University began to develop, in co-operation with the music teachers, a place in the musical life of the province. He also gave support to the Institute of International Affairs, the service clubs, the Canadian Club, the Y.M.C.A., and the churches found him ready to work with them in every way possible. Several times a day in below-zero weather he drove his car from the University to Winnipeg, a distance of ten miles, returning home often late at night. The physical strain of this was much heavier than it would be now, when snow-clearing and road-sanding are much more efficient than they were in the thirties. Only his enormous energy; his capacity to work eighteen hours a day; his lively sense of humour, his interest in and genuine liking for people, and the peace and security he found in his home with his family kept the man going in those first difficult years at the University of Manitoba.

Meanwhile, as was inevitable, the national organizations had discovered him and in 1938 he became President of the National Council of the Y.M.C.A., a position he held until 1942, when he resigned to become Chairman of the Canadian Youth Commission. He encouraged and was first Chairman of the National Film Institute. In 1942 at a conference of the Canadian Association for Adult Education he was elected President of that organization and gave it unique service and devotion for over two years. When World War II broke out he at once became chairman of the committee that set up lectures for the troops in Winnipeg, and it was this committee that framed the report on behalf of the Canadian Legion and the C.A.A.E. that became the basis of the Canadian Legion Educational Services which carried on in Canada and overseas throughout the war.

It was during those years that I myself began to know him and to cherish his friendship. Everyone who knew him intimately remembers his lively sense of humour, his quick wit, and the enormous gusto of his delight in a good story, particularly if the story had to do with Cape Breton. I remember spending an evening with him in a room in the Chateau Laurier, Ottawa, in 1941, just after he had completed two days or more of presiding at the annual meeting of the National Council of the Y.M.C.A. He was weary but relaxed and I told him the Father Jimmy Tompkins story, much too long to relate here, of "the Cape Breton molasses with the queer wild taste to it." We went on from that to James Gillis and the "Cape Breton giant," Angus McAskill, and the extraordinary story of his accomplishments. It happened that I had just come back from Nova Scotia and Cape Breton and had to tell him some of the new experiences I had had in his native country—about stopping my car to look over the lovely valley of the Margaree River which I knew to be one of the finest salmon streams in Canada. In a field near the highway was a lone farmer cocking up hay in the drying sunlight. I went over to talk to him. Like all Cape Breton sons of the soil, he was uncommunicative with "foreigners." I finally said, "Are there any fish in that stream?" He hitched his belt, stuck his fork in the ground, spat, then looking at me coldly, said, "God Almighty, man; there's times when it's fair agitated wit' fish." Then Sid told me about the Presbyterian minister at Mabou in the days when there was no love between Cape Breton and Nova Scotia who closed his Sunday morning service with a prayer ending, "We thank Thee, O Lord, for the sun and the rain that warms the crops and gives us harvest and for Thy compassion and love that brings salvation to us all, but most of all we thank Thee for the Gut of Canso that cuts us off from the wickedness of Nova Scotia." And so the talk went on, coming round to James Gillis' custom of footnotes to his love poems. In one of his verses he tells in tenderest fashion of the meeting of two young Cape Bretoners on the high plateau overlooking St. Ann's Harbour: the reader looks forward to a passionate ending but the poet shatters the illusion with this footnote: "And this field is noted to this day as the finest blueberry patch in all Cape Breton and is frequently visited in the summer by brown bears."

Four years after Sidney Smith became President of the University of Manitoba, he was invited to address a meeting of business men in Toronto. The Conservative party were at this time looking for a new party leader and shortly after his visit the *Financial Post* published an article in which the suggestion was made that the Conservatives might well take a look at this young Maritimer who had already done such "a remarkable job" at the University of Manitoba. There was little comment on the suggestion at the time, but three years later he made his first appearance as a political figure when he took part in the Port Hope "round table" conference of September 1942. Some of the planks he helped to formulate were adopted three months later at the party's Winnipeg convention, when the "Progressive" prefix was attached to the party name.

Meanwhile there had been a considerable build-up in the press for Sidney Smith's qualifications as a potential leader of the Conservative party. One of the most thorough and convincing statements was an article by Dana Porter, now Chief Justice of the Province of Ontario, in *Saturday Night*, October 18, 1941:

The teaching of Sidney Smith was such that its impact grew on the reflection of later years. His method was by no means popular amongst students whose chief desire was to pass examinations with the maximum economy of effort, but no man, no matter how apathetic, can entirely escape from the stimulating effect of repeated, disturbing contact with original and resilient intellectual power. . . . There is a widely held reserve towards any proposal to place an academic man in high places of responsibility in "public affairs". For academic men frequently become identified with certain doctrinaire theories. By the nature of their training they have limited experience in executive functioning and from the seclusion of their lives have little contact with the rough and tumble of the outside world. But the name of Sidney Smith has not sprung into political prominence by reason of any theory or any purely academic distinction. It is primarily the result of a brilliant constructive "practical achievement", broadly conceived and skillfully done. The qualities of leadership do not grow exclusively in any stereotyped channels. They may grow in any soil where creative enterprise may flourish and where tact and persuasion may bear full fruit.

It became apparent in 1941 that Sidney Smith was progressively under pressure to stand for nomination as leader of the Conservative party in Canada, but it was not until the Winnipeg convention that he agreed to do so and then only on condition that John Bracken, Premier of Manitoba, refused to stand. It appears from articles in the press at that time that the front runners for the position were: Sidney E. Smith, John Diefenbaker, Howard Green, the Hon. H. H. Stevens, and the Hon. George Drew, Premier of Ontario. John Bracken, mainly because he was the choice of the Hon. Arthur Meighen, then head of the party, seemed to have the best chance if he agreed to allow his name to come before the convention.

Bracken finally announced that he would accept if the policies laid down at the convention were acceptable to him. Particularly important to him was the change of name to Progressive-Conservative. There can be little doubt that President Smith was intrigued by the idea of leading the Conservative party in the next election, particularly because most of his supporters were agreed that it would eventually lead to the Prime Ministership of Canada. Nevertheless he kept his original resolve; he would run only if Bracken refused. When Bracken learned that his demand for a change of name had been rejected by the convention he refused to be a candidate for the leadership. But a resolution was hastily put through the convention postponing the change of name until after the leader had been chosen. Meanwhile Smith's name was put in nomination and his speech of acceptance was in his pocket. At 7:55, five minutes before the deadline for nominations, John Bracken appeared in the auditorium and accepted the nomination. Sidney Smith withdrew his name, tore up his speech, and apparently put the matter completely behind him. A letter from G. V. Ferguson, then editor of the *Winnipeg Free Press*, and now editor of the Montreal *Star* states: "Mary and I, Grant Dexter and Bruce Hutchison—all desperate Grits—met Sidney as we left the auditorium and asked him to the Dexter-Hutchison suite for supper. Rather to our astonishment he chose us over anyone else, and we had a gay party. Sidney behaved extraordinarily well. He must have been bitterly disappointed—had Bracken stood out Sidney might well have been a walk-in for there was quite an undercurrent in his favour but he didn't show a trace of this, talked coolly, cheerfully, and dispassionately of his ambitions and his hopes and readied himself to go back to his job. He seemed admirably adjusted." His only reported comment afterwards was "Well, I nearly got my fingers burned."

These brief but exciting excursions into the field of politics had in no way interfered with his major interest, the welfare of the University of Manitoba, but many of his best friends were opposed to his participation in political affairs. Dr. Norman MacKenzie, now President of the University of British Columbia and a life-long friend and colleague of Sidney Smith, says: "He was always interested in politics and would, I know, have liked to have been the leader of the Conservative party and the Prime Minister of Canada. Personally, I was opposed to this, particularly after he had established himself as an outstanding figure in the academic life of Canada. My opposition may have been in part selfish, and I would be the last to deny the importance of politics and of high office in politics, but as I often told him, he had acquired over the years a lot of experience in academic affairs; he had been a national figure and spokesman; and he was making a most important contribution to what I consider to be one of the most important vocations in the world."

Before the Winnipeg convention he had discussed with Walter Crawford, the Comptroller of the University and his closest friend, the suggestion that he accept nomination for the leadership of the Conservative party. "He asked me," Mr. Crawford says, "what I thought of the idea and I answered that I was surprised that he would consult as staunch a Liberal as myself on the matter. I then reminded him that, although still a young man, he had lived a comparatively sheltered life for fifteen or twenty years and I added, you are a man who loves people and all the small things that make up their daily lives. You do not want to hurt them, and you dislike going to bed at night if there is any rift between yourself and a colleague. Therefore do not touch politics; if you do, your opponents and sometimes your friends will throw everything at you but the kitchen stove and they may use the lids as well. He listened to me, but I could see he did not believe me. It was probably not until after his appointment to the post of Secretary of State for External Affairs by the present Prime Minister in September, 1957 that he realized I had given him good advice."

After the convention of 1942 Smith turned again with unaltered dedication to the affairs of the University. It had been apparent from the beginning of his administration that

new blood was needed in the teaching staff. The men who
had made the University respected and its standards note-
worthy were nearing the end of their service; new appointments were required if the University was to regain the
confidence and loyalty of the community it served. Two
appointments made in 1935 had helped greatly in that respect.
Professor Morton writes:

The first was that of the brilliant and urbane E. K. Brown of the University
of Toronto as Head of the English Department. . . . Brown was a *docteur
ès lettres* of the Sorbonne, a scholar's scholar, a critic of genius, a rare and
lovable personality and withal a shrewd faculty politician. His stay at
Manitoba was to be only too brief, as was, alas, his intense and laborious
life, but his coming shed on the university and faculty the radiance of a
first-rate mind and an absolute devotion to scholarship. The second appointment, that of Robert McQueen of the University of Saskatchewan, as
Head of the Department of Political Economy, was of like quality but of a
very different nature. . . . McQueen was not a first-rate scholar, though a
fine economic thinker. He was a personality, large, rugged and compelling,
of a philosophic shrewdness and welling humour that charmed his colleagues
and held his classes in thrall.[6]

The outbreak of war in 1939 brought new problems to the
University of Manitoba, as in fact it did to all the universities
in Canada. There was the inevitable loss of students and staff
to the armed forces. The call to arms meant that only excep-
tionally able students in the professional schools whose services
would be required in specialized fields and students in the
arts whose qualities as scholars would be useful in the total
war effort were exempt from immediate enlistment. But by
1942 it was necessary to begin planning for the post-war
years. The Federal Government was already at work setting
up plans for the rehabilitation of its returned soldiers, sailors,
and airmen. In this work the university presidents of Canada
played an important part. They and their associates were the
people who had intimate knowledge of the capacity of
Canadian universities to handle successfully and effectively

[6]*Ibid.*, pp. 160-1.

the demands of the post-war period and also had some idea of the cost. The educational programme carried on by the services in co-operation with the Canadian Legion had already revealed by 1943 the extent to which the universities would be called on to provide professional and general training. The Department of Veterans Affairs at Ottawa called on the university officials not only to assist in planning locally for the expected invasion of students but to help in the planning of the over-all programme of rehabilitation. In all this, President Smith played an increasingly important part. It had been the original proposal that the Department of Veterans Affairs should pay the tuition fees, plus a monthly allowance, to each veteran student. It soon became apparent the universities would need additional money to provide staff, classrooms, and equipment. Dr. Smith and H. W. Jamieson of D.V.A. worked out together the first draft of the supplementary grant scheme of $100 per academic year for each university student veteran. This was the forerunner of the present scheme of federal grants to universities.

In 1944 the University suffered two major setbacks. In January its great Chancellor, Dr. J. W. Dafoe, died; and its President was appointed Principal of University College, Toronto, with the understanding that one year later, after the retirement of Dr. H. J. Cody, he would succeed to the Presidency of the University of Toronto.

It was a deserved promotion from ten years of able service to the University of Manitoba. President Smith had found the University of Manitoba shaken and left it stable. His deft administrative touch, his geniality in all personal matters, the firmness and legal exactness in all matters of business, had made him indeed a reconciler of irreconcilables, a model administrator President.[7]

There were a great many official and informal farewell parties for the Smiths before they left Winnipeg, two of which were particularly impressive. There was a farewell

[7]*Ibid.*, p. 172.

luncheon at the Manitoba Club on July 25, 1944, given by the University Board of Governors. The address by the late Mr. Justice H. A. Bergman, a member of the Board, was an eloquent tribute to the ten years of dedicated service the President had given to the University. In the course of his remarks Mr. Justice Bergman outlined some of the problems the youthful President had faced when he had come to Winnipeg ten years before, and after paying a warm tribute to Mrs. Smith, who was unavoidably absent, he concluded:

I can assure you that none of us feels that you are running away from an unfinished job. The special problems which faced the University when you first came have been met and solved. The problems that now face the University are problems of the future which for the most part are common to all Canadian universities. You have visualized and anticipated these problems of the future, and the work which you have done by way of preparation to meet and to solve them will be of invaluable assistance to your successor and to the Board. . . . You would, of course, have made good in any surroundings, but there have been some local factors which contributed to your growth and success. While you were here you were teamed up with Walter Crawford during the entire period. I cannot imagine any two men more utterly unlike, but what a matchless team you have made. You were fortunate in working under a Board which gave you the greatest freedom of action and never interfered with you in any important respect . . . I would like to believe that you will find that Western Canada and the City of Winnipeg in particular, with their free and easy ways and their friendly atmosphere, have left their permanent impress on you. That Western impress will stand you in good stead in the more conservative atmosphere of Toronto and Eastern Canada. You will find that your ten years in Winnipeg have made you a broader-gauged and a better Canadian and better qualified to fill your new post.

There was also the official resolution of the Board of Governors. On both of these occasions Smith was deeply moved by the recognition of the work he had done during his ten years as President and by the warm and affectionate tributes to himself and his wife.

An occasion which filled him with particular delight was

the farewell dinner given in his honour by twenty-two of his personal friends. After the meal the chairman announced that there would be no speeches, but a topic of conversation had been chosen, namely, "Why it is a good thing Sidney Smith is leaving the University of Manitoba." Two penalties would be imposed: one on the first man who expressed regret at his departure, and the second—a much more severe penalty—upon anyone who referred, however remotely, to "the great job he had done at the University of Manitoba."

One of the happiest of the farewell occasions was a garden party given by the University staff. All the members of the working staff, including the girls in the residence, tradesmen, workmen on the farm and the grounds, were invited. They all came except Sam Morrison, the grounds foreman, who was unable to attend because the cleaners had ruined the only suitable suit of clothes that he owned. "Sam and Sidney were great friends," says Walter Crawford, "and the President was deeply disappointed at his absence. The girls from the residence all appeared in their best dresses and when they lined up to shake hands, Sidney performed one of those minor miracles of his—he called every girl by her first name without faltering. It was this endless fascination of his with all kinds of people that enabled him to do this sort of thing. At the time of the party, during a quiet moment, Sidney said to me, 'I probably have more friends among these people than I have among my academic colleagues.' "

So it was that President Smith and his family left Winnipeg in the summer of 1944 after ten difficult but rewarding and, for the most part, happy years, to undertake the most complicated and arduous job he had yet faced, the administration of one of the principal universities in the British Commonwealth. He was leaving behind him a job well done. He had in fact made a university out of a number of almost autonomous faculties. He had succeeded in having a new University Act adopted, which greatly extended the powers of the President, provided for the appointment of a Senate in place of the old University Council, and clarified and consolidated the business and academic organization of the University. There were also the new $50,000 library for the Junior Division, the establishment of a Faculty of Education, the improvement in pensions and the extension of the scheme to include all members of the staff, the enlargement of the university family to include Brandon College, formerly the property of the Baptist Church, the addition to the University of a Department of Extension, and the establishment of an Evening Institute which offered classes in a wide variety of subjects not leading to a degree.

It was in Smith's nature to accept the challenge of new responsibilities. He was constantly adding to his already heavy load of official duties by taking on such exacting tasks as Chairman of the United Church Pension Fund, Chairman of the Canadian Council of Christians and Jews, the Education Committee of the Army and Air Force, the National Council of the Y.M.C.A., and so on. This new challenge was the greatest of his career, and the thought of it filled him with delight. He came to Toronto an eager and a happy man.

CHAPTER THREE

Toronto Days

IN MANY WAYS COMING TO TORONTO WAS LIKE COMING HOME. During the five years from 1925 to 1929 when Sidney Smith had been a Lecturer at Osgoode Hall the Smiths had made many friends, and everywhere, on the campus and in the city, the new Principal of University College was greeted and welcomed by former students and members of the University teaching staff who had known him almost twenty years before. Besides, he was now a national figure, and had been for several years involved with national organizations whose headquarters were in Toronto or Ottawa.

When Smith took office as Principal of University College in the early fall of 1944, he moved into quarters which had been occupied by some of the most distinguished scholars in Canadian academic history, and was taking over from one of the most gracious and kindly of them all—the late Principal, Malcolm Wallace. From his desk in the Principal's Office he could look across the campus to Simcoe Hall and the windows from which he would soon look out as President of the University. He knew that with the end of the war the University would have to expand its services and equipment to accommodate the thousands of young men and women returning to civilian life after serving in the Army, Navy, and Air Force. He must often have wondered what the next decade would bring in the way of anxieties, pressures, and difficult situations. But his experiences during the past fifteen years as Dean of a Law School and President of a University had given him renewed confidence in his capacity for hard work, the soundness of his educational philosophy, and a firm belief in his ability to arrive at fair and acceptable decisions.

He was older now, more mature, more knowledgeable than he had been when he went to the University of Manitoba ten years ago. He had put on considerable weight, an extra chin, and was no longer the slim young man of Dalhousie days. But he was still a handsome and imposing figure, dynamic, youthful, and friendly. He knew more about his own limitations. Experience had taught him that no man in a position of great responsibility can be all things to all men and to "beware when all men speak well of you." He knew more about his own faults too. Walter Crawford had told him that his speeches were repetitious and warned him against speaking "off the top of his head." One of the professors at the University of Manitoba had said of him: "As a human being Sidney Smith is an enigma to many of us. He varies between excessive friendliness and excessive reserve in his attitude to the same people at different times and it's difficult to know why." But sometimes a man finds himself in a position where he has two reasons for everything he does, one official and the other personal. His friends and sometimes his family who think they are close to him often find that he is a million miles away in a world they cannot enter with him even if he wished them to. It has been said of Smith that on occasion he could be tough and ruthless, but he knew that a job of reconstruction often calls for drastic action and people get hurt. Men who are unfitted for their jobs have to be superseded or weeded out.

Only Sidney Smith's closest friends ever knew how sensitive he was and how easily he could be hurt. Speaking of this characteristic, "Caesar" Wright, Dean of the Law Faculty and one of the President's closest friends, says, "He was a complete extrovert on the surface but actually deeply introspective. He was hurt if you told him a speech was too long, too wordy, or if you kidded him about having an evangelical platform manner. Colonel Eric Phillips, Chairman of the Board of Governors, who admired him and loved him as most of us did, once described him as a man of 'complicated simplicity'—a capsule description which I liked and which I think Sid did also. Among other things he was worried about his acceptance among scholars."

This last comment called to my mind an evening I spent with Sidney Smith in 1944, after he had come to Toronto. The question of scholarship came up in conversation and Sid said to me, "You know they say the same thing about you that they say about me: 'You're good at your job, but you're no intellectual.' They say I'm a good administrator and in my own field a good scholar but I'm no intellectual. What the devil is an 'intellectual' anyway?" "I'm afraid I don't know," I said. "Perhaps it's a quality of mind. I do know that I once heard an intellectual described by a professor of English (I think he was quoting an Oxford don) as a man who could happily spend his life on a study of Tennyson's use of the comma."

Criticism always troubled Smith and gave him many sleepless nights, particularly if he had to be harsh with a colleague; but he often recalled the dictum of the British jurist who said, "I have made a covenant with myself never to allow affection to press upon judgment." "It is not impossible," he once said, "that there might be found in a university a member who is a charlatan or a fool. In such a case the guiding principle in dealing with him must be in the best interest of the whole institution." That he could accept criticism in good spirit is shown in a letter he wrote to Walter Crawford in 1954 when he retired after twenty-one years as Comptroller of the University of Manitoba:

In writing to you [he said], the kaleidoscope of ten of the happiest, yet the most arduous years of my life flashes past, with its brilliant tints of hope and the realization of hope, and with its dull greys and some black streaks of frustration and retreat.

We did not always agree. That is one of the things I admired in you; for as I moved into my forties I realized that the confidence and assurance of my thirties were not infallible. (Herein I invoke the power of the understatement.) So in saluting a savior of a sore and battered institution in the critical years during the three D's—a depression in the world, a drought on the prairies, and a debacle in the University of Manitoba—I thank you also for the postgraduate training you gave me.

In all modesty, I still believe that the compounding was not unhealthy for the University which we sought to serve with all our hearts.

Mark Twain once wrote that the American Midwest was a region where one man is as good as another and usually a damn sight better. That is true of our prairies; and in you my colleague, who always pulled more than his weight, and my friend who never failed or even faltered in integrity and loyalty, I find the proof of Mr. Samuel Clemens' dictum because you *are* a damn sight better.

There would be criticism, some of it bitter and some of it mocking, on this campus also. But what he had said on leaving Dalhousie would be true here: "I will . . . give of my best in fair thinking, square dealing, hard work, common sense and devotion to the institution and the community which she serves." He was, says Joe McCulley, Warden of Hart House, "a real product of this continent. A believer in the historic, pragmatic culture of this country. The main thing if there is a job to do is to get cracking."

In July 1945 when he became officially President of the University, Sidney Smith "got cracking." There were many trusted friends on the campus to whom he could turn for advice. C. A. "Caesar" Wright of Osgoode Hall days—now Dean of Law; Dr. J. A. MacFarlane—now retired as Dean of Medicine; and Vincent Bladen—now Dean of Arts and Sciences. A few years later, one of his closest friends, the Rev. Dr. E. M. Howse, moved to the city. Dr. Howse had been a friend of his Dalhousie days, had been his Minister at Westminster United Church in Winnipeg, had ordained him as

an Elder there, and was to do so later at Bloor Street United Church, in Toronto. "In fact," said Dr. Howse, "when I arrived in Toronto, Sid accused me of 'following him around.'"
It is doubtful if Sidney Smith ever shared himself more completely with anyone outside his own family than he did with Dr. Howse. "He was not," says Dr. Howse, "a deeply religious man in the conventional meaning of that word; rather his religion found expression in his sense of responsibility, his sense of duty. His inherent friendliness was always finding new ways of expression. Every spring he would spend a few days fishing with friends at a private club not far from Toronto. Always after such a trip, which was usually on weekends, he would send me a mess of trout as 'penance for being absent from my place on Sunday.'"

From the beginning, the demand for speeches and an opportunity to meet the new President was unending. As was his custom, he accepted every invitation he could, seeing in it an opportunity to get acquainted and to present the University's case before as large a public as possible. Almost every day the President addressed service clubs, institutes, Canadian clubs, Alumni groups, student societies, business men's banquets, church organizations, professional societies, women's organizations. And as newspaper reports of his talks appeared he could see the inevitability of repetition. Millions of speeches on the theme of education are made every year; not one in ten thousand has anything new or original to say.

All during the years of 1944–5 he had repeated his belief that "the battle for Democracy will not be over when the cease-fire sounds in Europe—the battle of ideals and ideas will go on. The emphasis placed upon science due to the war will swing back to a greater emphasis on the liberal arts. If we haven't a study of man's relationship to man, we can't have the proper leadership in meeting the problems that have to do with human needs." "Education," he said, "is more than an increased expertness; it concerns itself with man's moral as well as his intellectual development. The end of learning is not knowledge but virtue."

Speaking of the future of the University he declared, "Good appointments are not good enough; first-class ones are essential. Many Universities have been blighted by having too many merely good appointments and too few really excellent ones. The University which does not possess a reasonable number of first-class minds may be conferring degrees but is not imparting education." Dean Vincent Bladen, who had been a close friend since the President's Osgoode Hall days, comments, "He gave much attention to 'standards of entrance.' He was concerned to guarantee the presence of gifted students who might be excluded by poverty and to reduce the number of the dull uninterested students who would not and could not profit from association in the 'community of scholars.' One must notice also his determination to assemble a staff of not good but excellent scholars. He strove to make excellent appointments." In this connection Dean Andrew Gordon points out that "most of the senior positions in the University at the present time are Sidney Smith's appointments."

The press, with rare exceptions, enthusiastically approved his pronouncements. He had a flair for phrases suggesting headlines and his speeches made good copy. Papers throughout Canada applauded when he said, "Certainly there can be no place in a democracy for an aristocracy founded upon class and privilege, but there is a place for the aristocracy of talent; no better place than in the University."

There were times, of course, when he was belaboured by certain newspapers, such as the occasion in 1951 when at the Convocation exercises at the Ontario Agricultural College, he said: "Canada should get rid of the chip on her shoulder. Let us as a nation put more attention and effort into the translation of our democratic ideals into reality, and use, in that direction, the energy we now spend in being sensitive about the attitudes of other nations toward us whether it be the United Kingdom or the United States. Sensitiveness may betray adolescence, or it may well be a manifestation of our failure to be worthy of the respect of other nations." This speech called forth a barrage of bitter comment from the Liberal press and leaders of the Liberal party, for it was considered to be an attack on the Hon. Lester Pearson and a speech that he had recently made on Canadian-American relations. Senator David Croll recently told the writer, "We took him on about that—told him he was stooging for George Drew." Smith's only reply was "I'm going fishing with Mike in a few days."

As already noted, the President was at his jovial best on informal occasions. Often at dinner meetings, for instance, he was able to slough off an official bearing for a relaxed, even colloquial phrase but often one with point. Such an occasion was his meeting with the Eastern Section of the American Laryngological, Rhinological and Otological Society at the Royal York Hotel on January 31, 1957. After suggesting that their Society must be the most "logical" Society in the world, Smith announced that they had been utterly illogical in subjecting themselves to the dubious oratory of a university president, for university presidents are often defined as "pillars of brass by day and bags of gas by night." "You may be shocked to hear," he said, "that I believe you are doing your work too well. I believe that most people hear too much, smell too much, talk too much and swallow too much. There was a convention of the Conservative party in Winnipeg in 1942 and in the course of the speeches a man in the gallery stood up and called out, 'Use the loud-speaker, man, no one up here can hear you'. Immediately someone on the floor replied, 'Sit down and thank God you can't'. At the University Conservatory here they are constructing a radio telescope in order to listen to the radio waves from outer space. I gather that with their receiving apparatus they can tune in Venus and tune out Elvis. That is what we all need—some sort of selector knob with which we could tune out screaming commercials, discordant voices and tune in good music and good conversation."

The administrative burdens Dr. Smith assumed as President of the University were far heavier than anything he had ever borne before. In the two years which followed the end of the war the student enrolment jumped from approximately 7,000 to 17,700. It was obvious that there would have to be a change in the administrative establishment. Fortunately, the President had as his good friend and adviser during these difficult readjustments an able and astute executive in the person of Colonel Eric Phillips, Chairman of the Board of Governors. The combination of two such dynamic and experienced administrators was soon apparent in a more direct chain of command and a tightening of the system of federation under which the University operates. For many years the Bursar, with the finance committee of the Board of Governors of the University, had been in charge of financial matters. Among the changes made to meet the problems created by the population explosion on the campus was the appointment of a full-time Comptroller and, in 1948, an Assistant to the President (in this case, Dr. Claude Bissell who ten years later was to succeed Dr. Smith).

In 1945, in a desperate effort to provide housing and class-room accommodation for the incoming students, the President and Colonel Phillips worked out a plan for taking over a munitions plant at Ajax as a residential and teaching centre for engineering students. I remember hearing Sidney Smith refer to this undertaking once at a meeting with some friends, and he said with a grin, "We would have been away out on a limb if the students hadn't turned up. But within a year after that opening in January 1946, we had 3,000 students out there."

In an interview concerning this period, Colonel Phillips said to the writer: "Perhaps the most important achievement of Sidney Smith's career as President of the University of Toronto was to make all of us—the Board of Governors and the teaching staff—conscious of the necessity for unity. There were many diverse units in the federation which make up the University. Some of them were virtually *terra incognita* so far as the administration was concerned. We scarcely knew, for example, that the Royal Conservatory of Music belonged to the University or that we had anything to do with the Connaught Laboratories, or the Royal Ontario Museum."

I reminded Colonel Phillips that it had been said that he and Sidney Smith actually remade the University. He answered: "That is perhaps an overstatement, but it *is* true that Sidney and I, with great assistance from Henry Borden, undertook a complete reorganization of the administrative side of the University. This was vitally necessary if we were to build on a sound foundation, because it is no exaggeration to say there was practically no trace of any organized plan for the administration before this date. We had solid authority for the reorganization of the University. Too little credit has been given to the Royal Commission of 1906. This Commission under Sir Joseph Flavelle was charged with an examination of the affairs of the University and it is from its wise recommendations that the present University Act evolved. The Act imposes upon the Board of Governors the task of governing the University and at the same time the responsibility for the appointment of the President. The President with his academic colleagues is wholly responsible for the academic affairs of the University. Together with the Senate he develops agreed academic policies with the certainty that the selection of academic staff is, in the last analysis, his exclusive prerogative."

At this point I interrupted Colonel Phillips to point out that

I was having difficulty in making this profile of Sidney Smith anything more than a prolonged eulogy. Colonel Phillips replied: "He had his faults like anyone else, of course, but I would find it difficult to discuss them because I had a very great affection for the man. We were very close to each other for thirteen years and I never ceased to admire his enormous capacity for hard work, his fine mind, and his clever, if somewhat roundabout, administrative techniques. He always knew how to get his own way with his colleagues even when in committee one often felt like saying, 'Come on, Mr. President, let's get on with it.' He used to like to have his ideas and plans tested by his colleagues and in meetings of the Board of Governors or the Senate, he would send up trial balloons, which often confused and annoyed people who were not accustomed to his methods. But in the end one discovered that he always had a clear idea of what he was after and usually got his way. In my opinion he was a great university President."

Speaking of the heavy load the president of a large university has to carry, Dr. Murray Ross, now President of York University and for some years Assistant and Vice-President to Sidney Smith, said: "Perhaps the greatest hardship in such a position, especially for a warm and friendly person like Sid Smith, was that he could have only a few intimate friends and most of these he could only see on fishing trips or vacation.

"There were some sixty—Deans; Heads of colleges, schools, and institutes, student organizations, etc.—that the President had to deal with regularly. There were convocations, annual meetings, special reports, yearly publications, and handbooks of the students and Alumni, all of which required a greeting or a foreword from the President. All of them had to say something; but he was a great man for doing his homework and more often than not the finishing touches were put on a speech or a report at 3 o'clock in the morning."

"Every year," says Joe Evans, Registrar of the University

during the Smith régime, "we had to sign some 3,000 certificates. This operation required all day Saturday and most of Sunday. The man was tireless. When my arm would drop off he would grab a file of them from my desk and plow straight on. He always took four to five hundred home with him and probably sat up half the night to finish the lot. There were about 2,000 professors and lecturers on the staff and it was impossible to know them all; but he knew all about their qualifications and the work they were doing."

A young professor of my acquaintance, a member of the Forestry Department, illustrates this point again. "I drove him up to the Forestry Camp at Dorset one time and on the way up he made notes about the staff and the special work they were doing. When we reached the camp and he was introduced around, he never missed a trick. He had their names, their jobs, and in some cases even their youngsters' names fixed in his memory."

Principal Moffatt Woodside also gave me insight into Smith's habits as an administrator: "In making up the University Budget he mastered every item of it and discussed it with the Deans in turn. He would work on it over weekends in his office. Usually he would have lunch sent in for himself and those of us who were working with him but often he would forget all about it and work right through the afternoon. He knew the soft spots in a budget and exactly where trimming could take place, but he always insisted that if cuts had to be made they would be made in administration costs and not at the expense of the University's standards of teaching and research. Actually during his day, administrative costs at the University of Toronto were about the lowest in Canada. Although it is true that he had very little time for close friendship, it was surprising how much he knew about his staff— even the young ones, and he always knew what was going on on the campus.

"One of the things we discovered about Sid Smith after he had been here a few years, was his extreme sensitivity about any criticism of the University from any source—the public press or from his colleagues. Any attack on the University was like an attack on his family and it made him hot under the collar. When the 'Committee on the Rôle of the Humanities' in the University of Toronto was set up, the Chairman was Professor Harold Innis, but when Harold Innis became ill I had to take over as Chairman. In the draft report of the Committee, reference was made to the library of the University of Michigan and its superiority over the new University of Toronto library. This made the President extremely indignant and hurt and I, as Chairman of the Committee, was the first to bear the weight of his annoyance."

As soon as the pressures created by the end of World War II and the subsequent invasion of the campus by war veterans had subsided and the University was again a smoothly functioning organization, the long-contemplated changes in its permanent structure and policies began to take shape. In his first report to the Board of Governors, the President had stated that university salaries in Canada were out of line with the higher costs of living, higher taxation, and with the greatly increased remuneration of professors in the United States. He continued to urge in subsequent reports, and before public bodies, the necessity of a change in this situation. The result was that, between 1945 and 1957, there were five major salary increases for all members of the teaching staff. By virtue of these advances, the staff of the University of Toronto now receives stipends which are comparable with those paid by universities of equal status in the United States. These advances were followed in 1946 by a group insurance and pension plan for the academic staff, and a few years later a group insurance plan for the administrative staff came into effect. In 1955 these separate programmes were amalgamated in a new and comprehensive university pension and group insurance scheme which included readjustment benefits in keeping with the increased cost of living.

In his Annual Report for 1948–9, the President announced that the Pass Arts course would shortly be replaced by a new General course which would demand a much higher level of academic standing from students. It would, he said, include specialization in some particular subject, with a broad general programme in the more cultural subjects. On the same occasion he mentioned for the first time the necessity for remedial courses in English. "It is a sad commentary on the teaching of English in secondary schools," he said, "when many Canadian universities find it necessary to give remedial courses in English to university freshmen. But universities produce secondary school teachers. If those teachers are not liberally educated how can we expect a fine product from our schools? Mediocrity in the university breeds it in high schools."

In his opening address to staff and students that same year, he answered a question posed shortly before by a writer in a Toronto journal: "Is the university freshman of today brighter, better grounded in fundamental processes than his counterpart of 15 or 20 years ago? The consensus of opinion would seem to indicate that they are nothing like as good—academically speaking—as their prototypes of a generation ago." To this comment President Smith made a sharp retort: "Throughout history," he said, "youth was never, in the eyes of their elders, very promising. Since baldness, bulges, bifocals and bridges have a tendency to produce forgetfulness of the critics' own juvenile shortcomings, it is my opinion that you are better prepared than we of an older generation were." So he upheld his University on the campus, at public meetings, and on his visits to its graduates across Canada.

Continually he repeated his belief in the humanities as the bloodstream of a liberal education. He deplored the migration of graduate students to the American universities and urged more facilities and more money for scholarships. "The University of Toronto School of Graduate Studies," he said, in an Annual Report, "compares favourably with institutions of the first rank in Great Britain and the United States. But the 37 institutions which make up the Association of American Universities have an average of $100,000 each year to offer in fellowships and Canadian students are welcomed with open arms. In its best year, the Toronto graduate school distributed a little over $23,000—yet in this school the very hormones of universities may be secreted."

When students or graduates boasted that the University of Toronto is one of the largest universities in the British Commonwealth, he used to say, "So what! A university should never delight in the number of things—including students—it possesses; the only thing that makes a university great is scholarship." He had a genuine fear of academic elephantiasis and the degeneration of the university into a "multiversity."

Thus, before his departure in 1957, the new General course replacing the old "Pass Arts" course had been established; a new library had been built; the University Press had been greatly expanded; the School of Graduate Studies had been reorganized; salaries had been increased. There had also been the resolution of the question of legal education which had been a subject of controversy between the University and Osgoode Hall for seventy years.[1] The result was that at last the University of Toronto and all other universities in Ontario could, if they wished to do so, take their rightful and proper place in legal education. These were the items he listed when one of his friends asked him, just before he left Toronto, what he considered to be the major achievements during his twelve years as President. Nothing was said of the extensive building programmes, of the vastly enlarged enrolment in the student

[1]Senate resolution, Nov. 8, 1957.

body. As Dean V. W. Bladen remarked in an article in the *Canadian Forum*, "Mere bigness was not an attribute in which he took delight."

The best of President Smith's pronouncements appeared in his addresses to incoming classes of students or in his Annual Reports. To incoming students in 1953 he emphasized the tendency to standardization and conformity, and called on students to develop a critical spirit that can stand up against all "the dreary platitudes and pallid inanities that assail us." "I am not praising eccentricity for its own sake, but Canada could easily support more characters." He pointed out that "the most valuable member of society is the man or woman who has the capacity for dissent and sets up a resistance to mass movements and mass ideas." In his Annual Report for 1954 he urged that universities regain their spiritual leadership—they are today living on "the religious capital of their forefathers." "Religion should not be treated as an excrescence on the body academic. In a university of all places we must not neglect any area of human experience."

His last presidential report to the Governors and Senate of the University for the year ending June 1957 was in fact the sum of his thinking, the essence of his lifetime in education.

Ceaseless and relentless investigation in all domains of knowledge is a primary function of the University. History is changed by new discoveries and insights resulting from the creative and sacrificial efforts of university men and women to widen the frontiers of knowledge. We must protect and expand the opportunity for the members of our staff to pursue independent research. The professor's private library or laboratory ought to be an impregnable stronghold of the individual, as distinguished from the group; yet even here the battle must be joined against bureaucratism. The scholar of times past conducted research as his own interests and the logic of his discipline directed. If he were led into side issues, he would follow them and more often than not the sidetrack became in the end his main highway to discovery.[2]

[2]*University of Toronto, President's Report for the Year Ended June 1957* (Toronto, 1958), p. 11.

He then went on to point out how World War II had changed this individual pattern of research. Patriotism as well as poverty decreed that the scholar should shelve his own interests and turn to the immediate practical problems created by the war. There could be no question where the research scholar's duty lay in those years when national survival was in the balance. This changed pattern, he said, had persisted and now government agencies and foundations pay for a large proportion of the research work going on in universities, and in many cases the universities had relinquished control over the direction of research. Outside bodies asked for teamwork rather than individual effort, for planned and directed programmes rather than individual insights, for committees, for reports, and above all for "results." This, he pointed out, was having an insidious effect on university research. "Practical, applied research is an important public service which universities should not refuse to perform, but at the same time they must remember their more important duty to the lonely scholar whose inexplicable interest in a seemingly trivial question may lead to real advances on the frontiers of the subject."

Academic protocol could never quite contain Sidney Smith; his friendliness and gaiety kept breaking through and when he was away from it, he could revert to the boisterous, uninhibited, fun-loving person he had always been. He loved obstreperous people and used to ask, "Is he just a nice guy, or has he got something more? Does he belong among the 'goons and jiggers'?" On one memorable occasion when the Toronto football team defeated the University of Western Ontario, he danced a jig in the presence of 10,000 students and kissed the coach, Bob Masterson, on both cheeks.

"On fishing trips," says Dean Wright, "it was like living with a dynamo. He was the first one up in the morning and the last to bed at night, and the only time there was any rest in the camp was when he was out fishing, and even then you were never safe because sometimes he would upset the boat."

Dean Andrew Gordon confirms the picture: "His love of parties and boisterous fun was a delight to all of us. Every so often the President would entertain the Deans at the York Club; these occasions he referred to as the 'Deans' Brawls.' We had a lot of fun, of course, but they were extremely useful meetings. Inhibitions disappeared and we spoke frankly among ourselves and to the President. I always felt that in this way he got to know his senior colleagues better and learned a lot about their problems. Those of us who were lucky enough to be present will never forget a party Sidney gave for Sir A. P. Herbert when he was here a few years ago. They were both in great good form. The highlight of the evening came when Sidney and Sir Alan, both of whom were lousy singers, led the Assembly in singing 'The Foggy Bottom Blues' which Sir Alan had written as a somewhat scurrilous tribute to the late John Foster Dulles."

So the image of the man took shape in people's minds. It was a Rooseveltian image of homey friendliness and the deceptive charm of a man who nevertheless has iron in his fist when the occasion calls for it. Even the tilt of his head and the angle of his cigarette-holder contributed to that image.

There can be little doubt that there were repeated attempts behind the scenes to persuade Sidney Smith to enter the political field, but apparently he was not interested. There was much still to be done. During his years as President of the National Conference of Canadian Universities, together with Principal James of McGill University and others, he had been urging upon the Federal Government the need for larger subsidies for universities and a more generous provision of bursaries for graduate students. Besides, there was the huge building programme just getting under way on the campus. But with the Conservative landslide of 1957, the pressure increased and came to a dramatic head in September of that year.

The Chancellor of the University, Dr. F. C. A. Jeanneret,

tells the story: "On two different occasions after George Drew resigned as leader of the Conservative party, delegations from Quebec waited on him in his office and urged him to allow his name to stand for nomination as leader of the party, and promised him the support of the Quebec delegates including that of the Premier, Mr. Duplessis. He was amused when the leader of one of the delegations told him they had read through all his public addresses and could not find that he had ever at any time made disparaging remarks about Quebec or French-speaking Canadians. There were also delegations of Ontario Conservatives, but it was obvious that at that time he was not very greatly interested in such a proposal. When, however, in the summer of 1957, he was asked by Prime Minister Diefenbaker to accept the Portfolio of Secretary of State for External Affairs, he called a group of us together for lunch and told us about it. We all felt that he was excited about the offer and wanted to accept. In fact some of us had known for some time that he felt that he had done all he could for the University of Toronto, and felt that a change would be good for all concerned."

Sandy Forbes, who had been the President's friend and chauffeur for thirteen years, continues this story: "We drove down to Dartmouth University in New Hampshire where Dr. Smith and the Prime Minister, Mr. Diefenbaker, were to get Honorary degrees. We left on Wednesday, September 2 and on the way we took turns driving as we always did on long trips. He used to say, 'Okay Sandy, pull over to the side and I'll drive for a while.' Well, once when he was driving, I was talking to him about my family, and I mentioned that I had a sister living in New Hampshire not far from where we were going. So he said, 'Look here, Sandy, why don't you take the car when we get to Dartmouth and just get lost for a few days. Go and see your sister and take her for a drive around the country.' Well, I did that, and when I reported for duty on

Saturday afternoon, Dr. Smith said to me, 'You better sleep in my room tonight, Sandy, because we're going to start for home at daylight. I've been offered a new job and I want to get home to talk it over with my wife and my friends.' So we drove the 550 odd miles home next day. The P.M. and the President may have talked the matter over before, I don't know, but I feel sure that it was at Dartmouth that the thing was settled."

The news of the offer and the President's acceptance fell like a bomb on the campus and in university circles throughout Canada. There was general approval, some of it enthusiastic, in the press. But among Dr. Smith's friends there was sadness and some misgiving about his wisdom in accepting the appointment. His whole experience had been in the academic world. How would he adapt himself to the delays, the frustrations, and sometimes the humiliations of parliamentary life? His would be, too, a government department which is concerned with foreign policy, and the battle for men's minds is waged cunningly, ruthlessly, and seldom in the open. But this was a man who could never resist the challenge of undiscovered country. The blood of pioneers was in his veins and it was inevitable that he should accept.

Dr. Howse points out that he was, in an unconventional way, a religious man, and this new demand upon his life was in some inscrutable way a part of the "will of God" for him. It might be that he could do something to further the cause of peace in a frightened world. He took up his new work immediately and left for Ottawa on September 12. On November 7 the University Senate unanimously adopted a resolution proposed by Dean C. A. Wright, and seconded by Father Shook and Dean MacFarlane, expressing its profound regrets at his leaving the University, and containing a warmly eloquent appraisal of Sidney Smith as scholar and executive, but most of all as a human being.

"We are too close in time to pass a sweeping judgment that Sidney Smith was a 'great' University President, although many, indeed most members of this body, would not hesitate to so describe him.

"To many of his colleagues it appeared at times that he was unaware of the simple truth that the shortest distance between two given points was a straight line. Apart from the fact that a straight line is not a very interesting object in itself, and that long experience had taught him that in meetings such as the Senate anything that could add interest was an advantage, his friends have long ago concluded that the excursions and repetitions for which the President has become famous, were all a part of a basic plan. He was fearful that he should be accused of imposing academic policy from above, and anxious that at all times his colleagues should be informed on all matters of academic policy. There is no doubt that he frequently embarked on a complicated and tortuous voyage between A and B. When one appreciates that in so doing the monotony of the scenery was relieved, to say nothing of the fact that not infrequently such excursions gave time for many academic tempers to cool, who is there to criticize or even deprecate?

"What *is* important is that he was trusted by his academic colleagues; that he was respected for his integrity of purpose in the educational field and that the University of Toronto, an institution replete with centrifugal forces, during the twelve years of his presidency built steadily and truly on a sound academic basis, and stood always for higher standards in an atmosphere free from outside pressure of business or government—an atmosphere of scholarship and research."

The warmest tribute paid to Sidney Smith as a university president and a beloved colleague, came a year later when he was presented for a degree of Doctor of Laws, *honoris causa*, by Moffatt Woodside, then Acting President of the University of Toronto. "So long as there is anyone to record and remember and understand the history of the University of Toronto, he will be remembered with gratitude. So long as there is anyone to respect the University of Toronto he will be respected. So long as there is anyone, anywhere, who has known him, he will be respected, admired and loved."

So the Port Hood fisherman's son moved on into what was for him a strange new world—a twilight world, neither at peace nor wholly at war, where the tensions and daily anxieties of his office would call for all his stamina, his skill, his intelligence, and his capacity for prolonged hard work.

CHAPTER FOUR *End of the Journey*

ON SEPTEMBER 13, 1957, SIDNEY EARLE SMITH WAS SWORN INTO office as Secretary of State for External Affairs for Canada, the most difficult, demanding, and important post in the government. At sixty years of age he was embarking on a career for which previous experience had not prepared him. Because of his direct entry into the Cabinet at the Prime Minister's invitation, he was unable to benefit by the long period of apprenticeship as a back-bencher which most Cabinet ministers find invaluable. He was taking over his new job at a time when international tensions were as high or higher than they had been since the end of the war. The controversy over the Suez Canal affair had just ended. To make the situation even more difficult he laboured under the shadow of his able and world-renowned predecessor, Lester B. Pearson. From an educational point of view he was undoubtedly the most celebrated Cabinet minister in Canadian history, having been a Dean of Law, head of two large universities, and holding honorary degrees from eighteen universities in Canada, the United States, and the British Commonwealth. But, as one writer put it: "Sidney Smith literally had to go back to school again. The classroom was in the East Block. The lecturers were his senior officials, whose boss he was. The Course of Study was in the East Block documents. Perhaps he had never figured on having to learn his role in this way. But he realized that he must, and he did."[1]

However uncomfortable and strange he may have felt during his first weeks in the House of Commons, he was at home in his department. His associates there welcomed him with open arms; he was one of them, and in the tradition of his predecessor. One member of his staff said, "In spite of our affection for Mr. Pearson, there was absolute jubilation over Sidney Smith's appointment. All summer long we had had no full-time minister of external affairs; now we had one who could speak our language."[2] Soon after his arrival, he announced to his associates and let it be known to the Press Gallery that henceforth he would be called and referred to as "Mr. Smith." "It was characteristic of him that he put on no side, no new dignity, no air of unapproachability, in the East Block or in the House of Commons. He was as friendly to the office boy as to visiting dignitaries."[3]

There is a story that he went back to the House of Commons one night to do some work in his office and found that he had forgotten his key. He referred his problem to the security officer at the entrance desk, who said he could get a master key to let Mr. Smith into his office, if he had someone to guard the entrance during his absence. Whereupon the Honourable Secretary of State for External Affairs volunteered; he took over the sergeant's place of business, and during the next fifteen minutes answered several telephone calls and arranged to have taxi-cabs call for three private members. When the sergeant returned, Mr. Smith offered to "swap jobs with you any time."

His first appearances in the House of Commons, at the United Nations, and before the External Affairs Committee

[1]Norman Campbell in the *Ottawa Citizen*, March 18, 1959.
[2]There were many rumours to the effect that his staff in the Department of External Affairs were not co-operative and did not wish him to succeed. The author has not been able to discover any truth whatsoever in such reports.
[3]Norman Campbell in the *Ottawa Citizen*, March 18, 1959.

of the Commons, revealed him as painfully uncertain, both of himself and of his material. His colleagues in the Cabinet, some of whom only a few weeks before had been urging him to enter the political field, and had welcomed him warmly when he accepted the Prime Minister's offer, now regarded him with dismay. Here was a man whose policies in foreign affairs seemed to be in complete accord with those of Mr. Pearson. They questioned some of his statements and on one occasion he was contradicted on the floor of the House. It was part of his duty to establish the Conservative Government's policies in his department and wherever Canada was represented at international forums. This would not have been such a difficult task for a man of Sidney Smith's capacity if the Government he represented had been in power a long time. But some of his associates in the Cabinet were as inexperienced and confused as he obviously was himself during his first few weeks of office. This man had been through many tough battles, however. He took criticism in his stride, gave no sign of resentment, and remained his jovial and friendly self, knowing that given a little time he would get on top of his job as he always had done. To a friend he spoke the only comment he is known to have made on the situation, "Dief thinks I am getting better."

Within a few days of his appointment he had to make an important speech before the Assembly of the United Nations, answer questions in the House, appear before the External Affairs Committee of the Commons, and at the same time get ready for his own election campaign. After his election he attended a meeting of NATO in Copenhagen and from reports of that occasion, it was obvious that he was getting into his customary working pattern. One of his secretaries on return to Ottawa, said, "He wanted to work and discuss things all night. He never wanted to go to bed, and once when I crawled wearily to my room, he had been there before me and apple-pied my bed!"

Of this period, W. A. Mackintosh, the Principal of Queen's University, later wrote:

Before he was well out of the University of Toronto, he was in the Assembly of the United Nations and very quickly in the unfamiliar atmosphere of the House of Commons. He had had no experience of the working of the Civil Service and no direct knowledge of the complicated mechanics of government. The time was so short that he was inadequately briefed. For a period he appeared to falter. Obviously it is impossible for any political novice to settle into a department, get himself elected in an unfamiliar constituency, absorb the atmosphere of the House of Commons, and understand the complicated patterns and pressures of the United Nations in a matter of a month or six weeks. The atmosphere of a university should be, and usually is, one of friendly collaboration in achieving common interests. Certainly this was the atmosphere which Sidney Smith tried to achieve. The daily climate of both domestic and international politics is vastly more contentious and complicated. Collaboration there undoubtedly is, but it is streaked by a multitude of pressures, personal ambitions, vested interests, and traditions not readily unravelled by the newcomer.[4]

On November 4 he was elected to the House of Commons in Hastings–Frontenac and in the general election of March 1958 he was re-elected. Early in 1958 it became obvious that he was growing into his office and gaining a stronger grasp of its problems. The press and political observers began to get the impression that he was playing a larger rôle in the actual formation of foreign policy and taking a firmer stand in carrying it into effect. During these first months he followed his usual habit of reading all the fine print in any document from any source, and Harriet Smith admits that in many ways these were the happiest days of their married life, because her husband was at home at night more than he had been for years, and together in their Ottawa apartment they worked late at night, reading documents, *communiqués*, reports, and generally boning up on the new job.

The press during this period, although noting his lack of

4*Proceedings of the Royal Society of Canada, 1959*, 3rd series, vol. LIII (1960), pp. 130–3.

experience, was for the most part fairly charitable in its judgments. In an article in the *Globe and Mail* on March 19, 1959, Robert Duffy said:

In some respects Dr. Smith's political faults represented human virtues. On one occasion, caught off guard by a question in the House, he blurted out, "I am unable to answer." That was an honest statement. His more experienced colleagues on the Treasury benches might have made windy little speeches, pointing out how trivial was the information asked for, how great their other responsibilities, and thus preserving their alleged omniscience while promising to find an answer. Even during the worst period of Dr. Smith's hesitancy to answer directly for Canadian foreign policy, his unreadiness reflected what is normally a virtue of the academic mind—the unwillingness to analyse or give an opinion until all the background has been absorbed, the immediate facts digested, and a logical interpretative relation developed. This unfortunately is not the approach to political success. The political mind looks for certainty, a case to present—and all the rest is merely argument.

The French-language press, at the time of the Minister's death, was eloquent in its tributes to his life and to his growing strength as Secretary of State for External Affairs. In an article in *Le Droit* on March 19, 1959, Pierre Chalout said, "He believed profoundly that Canada's mission was one of peace. In the realm of politics which too often only rewards the mediocre, Sidney Smith, diplomat and intellectual, insisted on the possibility and necessity of coexistence between the East and the West. He believed that only good can come from the meeting of minds and insisted on the primacy of the spirit in a world devoted to the idea that 'The lion is king only because he is strong.'" In a lengthy review of Mr. Smith's career, on March 19, 1959, *La Presse* remarked: "His brief career as Minister of External Affairs, after a difficult début marked by much criticism, was soon followed by firm but flexible policies altogether diplomatic and always presented in the manner of the gentleman which always characterized him. His appearances at international conferences were such that he immediately won the respect of his colleagues of the diplomatic world, which today has lost an excellent apostle of peace." Dr. Hugh Keenleyside, then Director of the Technical Assistance Administration of the United Nations, speaking of his work at the United Nations, said, "Sidney Smith's relations with the other delegations at Headquarters and with the Secretary General were satisfactory from the beginning. His early difficulties were chiefly in Ottawa rather than New York, although he did show some lack of background and experience in the General Assembly. During the latter part of his service, however, I found that his own delegation staff were treating him with increased respect. They seemed to feel that he had ideas of his own and he was not depending so exclusively on communications with Ottawa. It was clear that the Minister was beginning to take command of the situation and that his staff was responding with pleasure."

The year of 1958 was one of constant overwork. He threw himself into the general election campaign in March of that year with all of his accustomed drive and enthusiasm. He addressed Conservative rallies, and supported candidates in every province of the Dominion, winding up the campaign in his own riding and in his native province of Nova Scotia. After the election the Minister returned to the routine business of his office. There was a trip to the British West Indies where, with the Hon. Mrs. Fairclough and the Hon. Mr. Churchill, he represented Canada at the inaugural ceremonies connected with the establishment of that new member of the British Commonwealth. During the summer months also there was much speech-making and careful preparation for the fall meetings of the General Assembly of the United Nations and other international conferences. In the summer he addressed a meeting of the "Churchman's Seminar on International Affairs" and made one of the most important pronouncements of his career as Secretary of State for External Affairs. The speech is of particular interest for two reasons. To begin with, it demonstrates clearly that in spite of changes in government, Canada's foreign policy remained substantially the same for, beneath partisan differences, there is a broad area of agreement on world affairs among Canadian people. Secondly, the speech is important because it contains the straightforward, unqualified statement that "The task of diplomacy is to preserve the peace." The speech read, in part,

The conduct of diplomacy among nations is a complex enterprise. It is extremely difficult to describe. Nothing is easier, of course, than to make fun of the profession of diplomacy. There are innumerable stories about the absurdities of protocol—(not a very important subject, I admit, until you make a mistake)—about the antics of the boys in top hats and striped pants, and so on. Perhaps I can risk reminding you of one of these rather slanderous stories since I do not see any striped pants in this audience.

Just after the first world war, half a dozen young men sharing a compartment on a European train were swapping stories about their wartime experiences and exploits on land, at sea, and in the air. Only one was silent. Finally, one of the group enquired politely where he had served during the war, and he was forced to admit that he had spent it behind a desk in the Foreign Ministry. "But just remember," he added waspishly, "if it hadn't been for us, you'd never have had your old war."

The story may be frivolous but its overtones are indeed sobering. The outbreak of war is the signal that diplomacy has failed; for the task of diplomacy is to preserve the peace.

I have been struck by the relation which exists between those who, like yourselves, minister to the moral and spiritual needs of mankind, and those who, by their pursuit of settlements of disputes among nations, are also engaged in and dedicated to the search for, on earth, peace and goodwill towards men. Our two callings have some requirements in common—requirements, I may add, which apply in equal measure to the profession of education. All three of them call for devotion to abiding ideals, for patience, hard work and refusal to accept discouragement. In all three groups progress is for the most part gradual, sometimes indiscernible, whether the aim is spiritual betterment, intellectual improvement, or peace among the nations. I know that in your vocation the value of unspectacular effort needs no underlining. It is the same in the conduct of foreign policy.

Herein is found in simple direct language, the essence of Sidney Smith's conception of his task as Secretary of State for External Affairs. Ever since he had taken over the department, the Berlin crisis had been a delicate and critical issue in foreign affairs, and Mr. Smith exerted every effort to prevent the Western powers from committing themselves to a rigid policy which would make compromise difficult if not impossible. In the speech he made in Halifax the night before his death, he said,

It is the first time since the war that we are witnessing a direct confrontation of the armed forces of the world's nuclear powers, with neither territory nor protégé states between them that serve to limit the scope and scale of possible hostilities. It is for this reason that the Canadian government has called for flexibility in the approach to the problem of Berlin—the kind of flexibility which would permit the Western powers to advance concrete proposals of their own without always being caught off balance by an interminable series of Russian initiatives. Surely there is room for firmness that would stop short of rigidity.

At the meeting of NATO in Paris, in December 1958, the Secretary played an individual rôle and insisted that the final *communiqué* should stress not only the West's determination to stand firm on Berlin, but also its willingness to negotiate with Russia on German problems. As a result of his guidance, the Canadian government later urged the Western powers to embark on a searching re-examination of the whole German question, to determine whether the accepted Allied policies were out of date.

Early in September 1958, he attended the Commonwealth Economic Conference in Montreal and addressed a large banquet given in the Queen Elizabeth Hotel by the Canadian government in honour of the vice-chancellors of the universities in the British Commonwealth. It was on this occasion that he introduced his plan for a regular annual exchange of Commonwealth university students. The suggestion was enthusiastically received by the delegates, and arrangements completed for a meeting at Oxford in the summer of 1959. On this occasion an organization to carry out the programme was established. References were made to Sidney Smith's vision in putting forth the idea. In its first year of operation, Canada sent twenty teachers abroad under the scheme, and we have in Canada 104 postgraduate fellows. An office has been set up in London to keep the programme functioning, and a second conference will be held in New Delhi in 1962. The plan is carried out in Canada in co-operation with the Technical Assistance programme of the Department of Trade and Commerce. Dean George Curtis of the University of British Columbia Law School was Chairman of the Steering Committee at the Oxford Conference, and is Chairman of the Selection Committee in Canada. Dr. T. H. Matthews, of Ottawa, at that time Executive Secretary of the Canadian Universities Foundation, is secretary of and mainly responsible for setting up the scholarship scheme in Canada. It is clear from the promises made at the Conference by Commonwealth delegations that the target of 1,000 scholarships and fellowships current at any one time has been attained and may soon be exceeded. Some delegations at the Oxford meeting were able to announce the number of awards to be made by their governments under the plan: the United Kingdom, 500; Canada, 250; Australia and India, 100 each; and the smaller countries in descending scale.

"After the banquet was over," says Chancellor Jeanneret, "Sidney invited a group of his old friends up to his room. It was a most happy occasion. At one o'clock, some of us felt it was time to go, but he insisted we stay on. At two o'clock we all felt he should rest, but it was actually about three o'clock in the morning when he came with us to the elevator, and when he said good-bye, the tears were running down his cheeks."

He went on from there to the Colombo Plan Conference in

Seattle, and then on a goodwill tour to Mexico and South America, visiting Lima, Rio de Janeiro, and São Paulo. On his return in December, he went at once to Paris for the NATO ministerial meeting.

At home again in Ottawa, the affairs of his department during the early months of 1959 called for study and decision. There was attendance at the House of Commons, Cabinet meetings, and the sessions of the General Assembly of the United Nations. All this meant endless homework and many sleepless nights. Pictures taken during these days show him smiling and apparently happy in the knowledge that he had found his place in what was to him a new world. But the strain of overwork and heavy responsibility was beginning to show in lines of fatigue and mental stress. There had been no real break in the heavy routine of duties. Mr. Henry B. M. Best, a member of his personal secretariat who had accompanied the Minister on his South American trip, reports: "He had had no holiday at all. Actually the Smiths had rented a cottage at Sharbot Lake in the Hastings–Frontenac constituency. They were never even inside it, although we did look through the windows one Sunday afternoon as we returned from the celebrations of the centenary of Stirling."

During the latter part of February and the first week of March 1959, preparations were under way for the visit to Ottawa of Prime Minister Macmillan and Foreign Secretary Selwyn Lloyd. It was expected that at this Ottawa meeting preparations would be made for a year of intensive diplomatic activity preparatory to an eventual summit review of the cold war, with particular attention to the crisis shaping up over Berlin. In fact the day-long stopover in Ottawa by the British Ministers on their way to Washington, was arranged for the purpose of bringing the Canadian government up to date on the outcome of the British leader's talks with the Russians, and subsequent discussions in Bonn and Paris on the position the Western powers should adopt. Mr. Smith had been under the care of two doctors for about a fortnight and was running a slight temperature, but he appeared to be in no real difficulty and refused to stay in bed or to rest during the daytime.

Meanwhile he had a long-standing engagement to address the twenty-eighth annual dinner of the Halifax Board of Trade on March 16. It was a happy circumstance that one of his closest friends, Professor George Wilson of Dalhousie University, was in Ottawa at the time and arrangements were made that they should make the trip to Halifax together. The story of that last train trip is best told by Professor Wilson:

"I met Sid in his office in Ottawa on the afternoon of Saturday, March 14. He had made all the arrangements for our trip to Halifax together. He had with him a young man to whom I took a great liking, called Duckworth. On the trip, Duckworth kept saying that the Minister ought to have come in a private car. Sid laughed and said that Halifax was the last place in the world where he would want to appear in a private car. It might do in other parts of Canada but not in Nova Scotia. We had dinner together and then Duckworth went off to his room. Sid and I then talked till past two o'clock in the morning. He satisfied me absolutely on certain points. He had no regrets about leaving Toronto and coming to Ottawa. He said that he had had a difficult time at first, the work was new and he had not had the necessary time to work into the job. The papers and the public generally had been critical. He was aware of all that, but he assured me that he was certain that he was through the worst. Give him another six months or a year and he would really begin to enjoy his work. He had felt all along that Canada could play a very useful rôle in the foreign affairs of the world, but he said that he had already learned one very important lesson—he had greatly reduced his expectations of the amount of good that he could do. It was very little that any individual or any nation could do in this stubborn world.

He had hoped to do much; he would be satisfied if he could do a little. I wanted to know if he [Sid] had felt that Mr. Diefenbaker had given him his full support. Sid assured me in the most convincing way that he had the greatest confidence in and even affection for the Prime Minister. I was surprised to hear how intimate and how united they were in their hopes and in their fears. I had often joked with Sid about his rather evangelical Methodist background. He now assured me with a laugh that he and the P.M. shared this weakness. They were not cynics, they did not despair of doing some good in the world. 'If that is naïve,' he said, 'then I want to be naïve.'

"And so the talk went on till long after midnight. It became very candid and very intimate. The brevity of our lives, the depth of our ignorance, how little good any of us can do—so the conversation went on. We had often talked of such things before. We did not realize that this was the last talk we would ever have together."

The Minister spent the time between his arrival in Halifax on Sunday afternoon and the time for his speech on Monday night with his sister, Mrs. T. Harold Johnson; he saw many old friends and went over the notes for his Board of Trade address. He always enjoyed his return visits to Halifax. It was like coming home again, and as he took the platform for what was to be his last public appearance, he appeared to be in excellent health and good spirit. The gist of his address emphasized the international importance of distributing the world's resources to meet the needs of expanding populations. He said, among other things, that he was more concerned with fighting Soviet expansion on the economic front than in the military aspect of the cold war. The speech was extremely well received and the Minister went home that night to his sister's house happy and relaxed. After breakfast next morning, he took a plane to Ottawa, arriving home about noon. Mrs. Smith was not at home, and he informed the housekeeper that he would rest a while before going to the House of Commons at 2 P.M. When Harriet Smith came home shortly afterward, she went into the bedroom to speak with her husband. He was lying on the bed with the glimmer of a smile on his face, but a massive cerebral haemorrhage had taken him quietly away.

Within an hour the news of the Minister's death had reached the House of Commons, and at 3 P.M. on the afternoon of March 17, 1959, the Prime Minister, in a voice shaking with emotion, announced to a shocked House that the Honourable Minister for External Affairs had died suddenly, and he suggested that the House adjourn at once. A few minutes later the Chamber was empty.

The news of the Minister's death came as a shock to the whole English-speaking world, and editorial comment at home and abroad unanimously praised Mr. Smith's work as of growing significance in international affairs. Stanley Burke, reporting from the United Nations, said that "The reaction to the death of Sidney Smith was most effectively expressed in the comments of the delegates as they met in the corridors, executive offices and the lounges of the United Nations building. The Secretary General described him as 'a sincere and devoted friend of the U.N.' Despite his brief career he had made useful contributions behind the scenes on disarmament, and on the delicate discussions that went on during the Lebanon crisis. But above all he made a reputation as a man of charm, intelligence and sincerity."

In announcing the Minister's death, the Prime Minister referred to him as "the happy warrior." This was a felicitous phrase. It was, I think, Oliver Cromwell who once said the happy and invincible warriors were those who "knew what they were fighting for, and were happy about what they knew." Sidney Smith had always known what he was fighting for and he was a happy man.

The funeral took place in Chalmers United Church on Thursday, March 19. The Governor-General, the Cabinet, and members of the House, Senate, and diplomatic corps joined hundreds of Ottawa residents in paying tribute. The service, notable for its dignity and simplicity, was conducted by the Rev. Mr. Leslie Griffiths, and the eulogy was given by the Minister's old friend, the Rev. Dr. E. M. Howse. It was a state funeral without pomp. Only the uniformed guard of honour, the pall-bearers, and the Band of the Royal Canadian Air Force gave it a national character. The psalms and hymns were the old familiar ones dear to the hearts of Protestants wherever the English language is spoken: "Unto the hills around do I lift up/My longing eyes," and "O God our help in ages past." Dr. Howse's tribute was the warm and heartfelt eulogy of one friend to another.

In Divinity and Love what's best worth saying can't be said—and here again what's best worth saying would break through language and escape. He was my friend and of deliberate intent I shall not seek the luminous phrase, the glowing metaphor which might etch upon our inward vision the eminent man whom we now mourn. He was my friend, and no tribute to his high talent is more worthy of remembrance than that among this catholic assemblage of those who pay tribute to his distinguished service, so many others can join with me in that proud litany: He was my friend. His unexpected death at the moment he was moving fully into his labour is a heavy tragedy for Canada and for humanity. But at least he fell on the field. Not his to know the faded light of dwindling years. Not his to count his final days an appendix in small print to greater deeds. As Dryden says,

> And could we choose our time, and choose aright
> 'Tis best to die, our honor at the height.

So he waved farewell, his honor at the height. And he passed from those he loved to "the starlit strip between the companionship of yesterday and the reunion of tomorrow."

> No further seek his merits to disclose
> Or draw his frailties from their dread abode,
> (There they alike in trembling hope repose)
> The bosom of his Father and his God.

After the service the body of the Minister was taken to Uplands Airport where it was placed on an R.C.A.F. plane for Halifax. The plane bearing the Minister was followed by another carrying Mrs. Smith, their three daughters and friends. The following day, after a brief service, Sidney Earle Smith was put to rest in the lovely old cemetery in Windsor, beneath a great maple tree and beside the graves of his father and mother. The Cape Breton boy who had travelled far and with great distinction, had come home at last to the land he had always loved.

In his Annual Report to the University of Toronto in June 1959, Dr. Claude Bissell, successor to Sidney Smith as President of the University, paid eloquent and moving tribute to the man he had worked with for many years:

Few men lived more fully. He had a restless and energetic mind that made him a sojourner in every area of human thought, and he had a warm and exuberant nature that gave him immeasurable resources for friendship. The great mark of the man was his persistent but kindly curiosity about people, events and ideas. The university was his life. Within a few years of coming here, he had raised most of the fundamental problems, and by the time that he left he had solved a good many of them. His twelve Annual Reports constitute the most detailed and at the same time the most illuminating accounts of the life of the University that are available to us. Under him the University was a happy and self-confident community. By his public addresses and his vigorous leadership, he brought new lustre to this University, and he spread its fame more widely than ever before. Although at his death he was a member of the federal Cabinet and a public figure, he will be remembered always primarily as a university man; and we at Toronto will join with his colleagues at Dalhousie and Manitoba in placing him among our illustrious great. The pity of his sudden death was that he had not yet had time to make his full impact in the new arena. But already his influence was beginning to be felt, and his voice was being raised in that courageous and outspoken way to which we had become accustomed. The typical accent was already there—that combination of shrewd legalism, warm feeling, and an idealism that grew out of his devout Christian upbringing and that reflected the simple and unpretentious democracy of Cape Breton where he was born, and to which he returned so often for rest and renewal. He left a mark upon his time and upon his country that the passage of the years will further illuminate.

Lightning Source UK Ltd.
Milton Keynes UK
UKHW010014210722
406167UK00002B/459